JESSAMYN WEST

(TUSAS) 192

JESSAMYN WEST

By ALFRED S. SHIVERS

Stephen F. Austin State University

TWAYNE PUBLISHERS

A DIVISION OF G. K. HALL & CO., BOSTON

my wife Clare Ann

unstinting love and understanding

Professor John Henry Groth

as a teacher of force and charm, he gave to studies

a kind of glory and made the past live again

Contents

Preface

T HE READERS I have in mind for this first study of Jessamyn West, who is one of the great living American fictionists, are those who want an accurate synoptic and objective analytical study of such works as *The Friendly Persuasion, Except for Me and Thee, South of the Angels, Cress Delahanty*, and others. But, at the same time, I make no pretense of stating the "last word" about this author concerning whom no extended biographical or critical treatment has hitherto existed. The book begins with a biographical chapter taking the career of Miss West up to late 1970. In what sense Jessamyn West is an "unconventional Quaker" author will be discussed only incidentally, or via indirection; for the major concern of this chapter is the relation of her life and times to her art. We may safely claim, as I do, that any Friend who devotes most of his or her talent to composing secular stories that are not overtly spiritually improving would *have* to be to that extent unconventional. That Miss West deals frankly with sexual matters is another point, one that alienated some of her sectarian readers—hopefully, only the narrower ones—after the publication of *The Witch Diggers* and *South of the Angels*.

The next three chapters consist of practical criticism, all mine unless otherwise indicated, plus summaries of the best of what little criticism has been written about her literature, whether by reviewers, explicators, or Miss West herself. In Chapters 2 and 3, I treat her work as related to two distinct geographical regions, the Midwest and the California seaboard. With the exceptions of the late books *Leafy Rivers* and *Except for Me and Thee*, this division also follows, in general, the publication sequence. The division shows Miss West as working forward in time scheme: *The Friendly Persuasion* begins around the middle of the nineteenth century; *South of the Angels* brings the reader to World War I; and *A Matter of Time*, the next-to-the-last volume discussed, has its surface plot in the present. My study shows West as being equally at home in the two regions.

As the plan of this study in literary criticism is to deal almost exclusively with that fiction readily available in West books, for the most part her best work published to date, the various stories in the journals never yet collected or reworked into book form are for the most part omitted here. Among these omitted ones are some designed, like "There'll Come a Day," mainly for the pulp-fiction market. The study devotes relatively little attention to Miss West's single venture into operetta (*A Mirror for the Sky*), and it does not concern itself at all with her poetry, comprising slightly over two dozen published items, all of which are quite short and none of which is as yet collected and readily accessible to the average reader. Her autobiographical and philosophical writings (*To See the Dream* and *Love Is Not What You Think*, respectively) are discussed only as they contribute to the biographical sketch and to the criticism that follows.

Since this book is about an author in whose life and work Quaker-ism has a special role, it would be useful and fitting at this time to say a few things about the history of the sect in American letters, including how Jessamyn West relates to it. The relatively tiny Religious Society of Friends, formed in England during the seven-teenth century, has generated in America a correspondingly small number of literary artists who have achieved national or world fame. But, when we consider that the Friends have always constituted a minority group in this country, that *The World Almanac and Book of Facts 1971* lists their number for 1970 at 126,219 as com-pared with over 204,000,000 of general population, it is easy to account for their scarcity among the famous; yet they have cer-tainly done well in relation to other minority groups of similar size in America. Doubtless their numbers in belles lettres are suppressed by the Quaker belief that any member gifted with language ought to employ that talent more or less exclusively to the benefit of the church. John Woolman's *Journal* (1774), a spiritual autobiography in plain, unadorned style, is a beautiful model which a member of the faith might be expected to emulate.

We find in the eighteenth century at least three Quakers, born in America, whose writings demonstrate distinct literary flavor: the humanitarian Woolman, already mentioned; the darling of the English Romantics, William Bartram; and the novelist of Gothic romance, Charles Brockden Brown. In the keeping of journals and the choice of so-called useful or practical subject matter, Woolman and Bartram followed in a long tradition of Quaker practice. How-ever, Brown as a literary man seems to have been more influenced by the books of William Godwin, Samuel Richardson, and Mrs. Ann Radcliffe than by his own Quaker upbringing.

Preface

John Greenleaf Whittier, of a later period, long held the reputation of being one of America's foremost poets, although his absorption with Abolition and his stylistic virtues of directness, simplicity, and emotion have regrettably run afoul of a new fashion in contemporary criticism. Few students of American letters would question that in Walt Whitman the Quaker influence at last reached greatness. Although not formally a Quaker himself, he had Quaker parentage, grew up in a section of Long Island where Quaker influence was pronounced, took an admiring and prolonged interest in the evangelist Elias Hicks, and introduced into *Leaves of Grass* ideas, terminology, and techniques which are often strikingly consonant with traditional Quakerism. Like the Friends, he insisted on getting firsthand experience ("You shall no longer take things at second or third hand, nor look through the eyes of the dead. . . .") Also like them he numbered the months, such as "Fifth-month" for May. We may also detect in his poetry a chantlike rhythm—he actually called his poetry *chants*—characteristic of most Quaker preaching of his era. Jessamyn West asserts in *The Quaker Reader* that there is little in *Leaves of Grass* which does not reflect Quaker influence.

As for the interesting minor Quaker *literati* of the present century, such as Daisy Newman, Janet Whitney, Elizabeth Gray Vining, Logan Pearsall Smith, Nora Waln, James Baldwin (1841-1925), and Maud Robinson, I will have occasion in this book to mention only the last two. Of all these listed, including Brown, there are clearly no world-famous Quaker practitioners in the medium of the short story or stage drama (play, opera, operetta). (Brown's novels, e.g., *Wieland*, were appreciated abroad, especially by John Keats, Percy Bysshe Shelley, and Sir Walter Scott.) Jessamyn West is probably the first Quaker author working in the media of the novel *and* the short story to gain an international reputation as well as the approval of serious readers.

ALFRED S. SHIVERS

Stephen F. Austin State University
Nacogdoches, Texas

Acknowledgments

Had it not been for the liberal cooperation of Miss West in providing biographical data, books, galleys, family papers, a writing notebook, photographs, help in locating obscure stories, and written explanations of her artistic aims and methods, this study could not have been written. But whatever faults exist in it are strictly my own. To offset the risk of overinfluence from my chief supplier of information, I have never forgotten to take an independent stand in interpretations and conclusions. In the same spirit, I have carried out a fairly exhaustive inquiry—in published materials, it was exhaustive—and tried wherever possible to check one source against another. In April, 1966, I made a special visit to the area about North Vernon, Indiana.

Many are the correspondents to whom I am indebted for aid, especially as so little has been published about the author and her work. Of prime service for various biographical details are the memoirs of her former teachers, relatives, friends, and acquaintances: Dr. William T. Boyce (Claremont, California), President Paul S. Smith (Whittier College), Mr. Merritt T. Burdg and Mrs. Olive Marshburn (both of Whittier, California), Mrs. Gladys Gauldin (La Habra, California), Mrs. Esther L. Mendenhall (Santa Ana, California), Mrs. Allie Clark and Mrs. John Woolf (both of North Vernon, Indiana), Mrs. Hellen Ochs (Columbus, Indiana), Mr. Richard Scowcroft (Stanford University), President of the United States Richard M. Nixon (Washington, D.C.), Mrs. Sue Lucas and Mr. Donald Kelly Lucas (both of Earp, California), and one relative who has requested not to be listed here.

I am particularly grateful to Mrs. Lois C. McClure (formerly librarian at the William T. Boyce Library, Fullerton Junior College, Fullerton, California) for much information about Jessamyn West's student life at Fullerton, to Mr. Donald C. Johnson (University Library, Northern Illinois University) for reproductions of early stories and for help in tracking down out-of-the-way periodicals, to Mrs. Lorraine Hartwick (Milwaukee Public Library) for statistical data, to Mr. E. M. Adams and Miss Jan C. Todd (Paul L. Boynton Library, Stephen F. Austin State University) for interlibrary loan materials, and to the officials of the Library of Congress for xeroxed stories and bibliographical aid.

Acknowledgements

For financial and secretarial assistance I am indebted to Stephen F. Austin State University and Northern Illinois University. For reasons too various to single out here I also owe a note of thanks to Dr. Edwin W. Gaston, Jr., and Mr. Edwin D. Shake (both of them friends and colleagues of mine at Stephen F. Austin State University); to Dr. Hensley C. Woodbridge (Southern Illinois University, Carbondale); to Mr. Ralph D. Olive (my dear lifelong friend on the *Milwaukee Journal*); to Mr. Horace W. Robinson, the director of the University Theater, and Mrs. Wilhelmina Bevers, the business manager of the University Theater (University of Washington); to Mrs. Ozella Dew (Tyler, Texas); to Professor D. Elton Trueblood (Earlham College); to Mr. Julian P. Muller (Harcourt, Brace & World); and to Mr. Henry Volkening (Russell & Volkening, Inc., New York City).

I wish to thank Harcourt, Brace & World for permission to quote from the books of Jessamyn West, and of course the author herself for permission to quote from the letters and other unpublished documents.

Not least, I am obligated to Dr. Sylvia E. Bowman, whose editorial labors have improved the book substantially.

Chronology

1902 Mary Jessamyn West born (July 18) near North Vernon, Indiana, daughter of Eldo Roy and Grace Anna Milhous West.

1909 In April, West family moved to Los Angeles County; settled briefly on orange ranch; within two years, moved to nearby Yorba Linda.

1914 Summer opening of public library in Yorba Linda—beginning of her "adult intellectual life," Jessamyn says.

1919 After graduation from Fullerton High School, attended Whittier College for one year.

1920- Fullerton Junior College.
1921

1921- Whittier College again; graduated with bachelor of arts,
1923 major English. On August 16, 1923, married Harry Maxwell McPherson.

1924- McPhersons moved to Hemet. Jessamyn secretary for school
1929 one year, followed by four years as teacher in one-room public school. In 1929, attended Oxford University for summer session; visited Paris.

1929- Graduate student at University of California. In August,
1931 1931, following tuberculosis hemorrhage, entered LaViña Sanitorium. Long period of "horizontal life" ensued.

1933 In November, joined husband in Yuba City, where he was vice-principal of high school. "99.6" written here.

1934- To Mt. Shasta, where McPherson was principal of high
1935 school.

1936- To St. Helena, where he was again principal. Published first
1940 short story, "99.6," in *Brown's Nutmeg* on June 10, 1939.

1940 To Napa, present home, where McPherson Superintendent of Schools.

1945 First collection of stories, *The Friendly Persuasion*.

1948 Operetta, *A Mirror for the Sky*, based upon an idea by Raoul Péne duBois. *The Pismire Plan* (science fiction novelette) published in *Cross Section 1948*.

1951 First novel, *The Witch Diggers*.

1952 A speech, *The Reading Public* (privately printed).

1953 *Cress Delahanty* (stories).

1955 *Love Death and the Ladies' Drill Team* (stories). Nine months of script writing in Hollywood.

1957 Indiana Authors' Day Award for the preceding book. *To See the Dream*, autobiography covering the Hollywood experience.

1958 Thormod Monsen Award for *To See the Dream*. Saw staging, May 22-24, of *A Mirror for the Sky* in Eugene, Oregon.

1959 *Love Is Not What You Think*. Death of mother, Grace West.

1960 Second novel, *South of the Angels*.

1962 *The Quaker Reader*.

1963 Death of sister, Carmen.

1966 Third novel, *A Matter of Time*.

1967 Fourth novel, *Leafy Rivers*. *The Chilekings* (science-fiction novelette originally published in a collection as *Little Men*).

1969 *Except for Me and Thee*—more "Friendly Persuasion" stories.

1970 *Crimson Ramblers of the World, Farewell*. Death of father, Eldo Roy West.

CHAPTER 1

An Unconventional Quaker

IT seems miraculous that Jessamyn West, who narrowly escaped suicide at college, who was considered an "incurable" at a tuberculosis sanitorium, whose Quaker heritage clearly forebade using one's talents for belletristic purposes, and whose family background contained no artists or theatrical folk of which we have record, should survive to pen a series of popular books which have been translated into at least nineteen foreign languages. Moreover, some of these books have few rivals in American literature for sheer artistry.

This improbable Jessamyn West was about thirty-seven when she wrote her first story, and she was almost forty-three before she published her first book—a time of life when most of those who have yearned to write have metamorphized into teachers, editors, and newspapermen. To chronicle her life, obviously an inspired one, is to risk perpetrating an injustice if the study is necessarily as brief as the present one. Also, to write the biography of the living means perforce to be limited, for the career of Jessamyn West is by no means over. Perhaps in this task so fraught with peril it is best to begin with her forebears.

I Forebears

Of the ancestry of Miss West's father, Eldo Roy West, relatively little is known, but his family seems to have been predominantly English.[1] Eldo West's mother was a Clark, a woman tall, dark, and gaunt, who relished fishing and who had an Indian spouse's conviction that her husband should do no household chores. Family history has it that the grandmother of this particular Clark was the Indian "blanket wife" of George Rogers Clark, the hero of the Battle of Vincennes. Eldo West, born in Indiana in 1879, grew up on a farm under fairly meager circumstances. Evidently far more intelligent than his nine years of formal education indicated, he taught school in Indiana and achieved relative prosperity in various kinds of work in California.

Grace Anna Milhous West, the mother of Jessamyn, came from a background of Welsh, Scotch, and, particularly, Irish people. The Quaker family of Grace's father sailed from Timahoe, Ireland, in the early eighteenth century to settle in America. A member of this Milhous line then married a Welsh woman of the Griffith patronym, who had voyaged to America on the same ship that had carried William Penn. The genealogy from this stage onward includes such families as the Prices, the Sharps (Irish), and the McManamans (Scotch-Irish)—all thrifty landowners, nurserymen, teachers, or preachers.

Jessamyn's great-grandmother, Elizabeth Price Griffith Milhous, was a Quaker minister who suggests by religious calling and name (but little else) the Eliza Millhouse of the early magazine stories in the *Friendly Persuasion* group. Her nurseryman husband, Joshua Vickers Milhous, is chronologically the "Jess" of *Friendly Persuasion*. This Joshua, along with his twin sister, were the youngest in a family that resided near Mount Pleasant, Ohio. When twenty-seven, Joshua journeyed into Pennsylvania and returned with his bride, Elizabeth, who in due time bore him eight children. In 1854, after the birth of his sons Jesse and Frank and of a daughter Edith, he moved with his family to Jennings County, Indiana.[2] One of Frank's descendants was Richard M. Nixon, who became president of the United States.

Jesse G. Milhous wisely chose as his bride Mary Frances McManaman, an educated lady blessed with glad spirits and energy, who, according to her famous granddaughter, was more or less the model for the Eliza of *Friendly Persuasion*.[3] To this couple, Grace Anna was born in 1884 near Butlerville in Southern Indiana. Her father ran the Maple Grove Nursery and raised for sale and for the family a veritable cornucopia of fruits.[4] Grace later took sensuous delight in recounting this abundance to her daughter, along with divers anecdotes that ultimately helped her re-create for herself and millions of other readers the vanished wonder of the past. Jessamyn, endowed with a rare sensitivity, heard in the mother's lonely yearnings suggestive hints—mere wisps of story situations—and was capable of turning them into literature.

One of Grace's memorable experiences at the age of sixteen or seventeen was to spend a winter on the County Farm about five miles south of Vernon, where her stern grandfather, blue-eyed and snowy whiskered James McManaman, was then superintendent. This "poor farm," as the neighbors called it, whose inmates—the derelicts, the paupers, the feeble-minded, an insane old woman, a former schoolteacher turned kleptomaniac, sexual offenders, to say nothing of a certain red-headed housekeeper and cook who was getting "betrayed" (as she preferred to call it) with embarrassing frequency—so horrified and fascinated the impressionable Grace that she continued to relate stories about the bizarre place and people to her children.[5] This "poor farm" became the setting for *The Witch Diggers*.

At twenty-one, Eldo Roy West married Grace against the objections of her parents, who eyed him as a non-Quaker of little worldly means, or promise, who was presumptively trying to marry into a well-established Quaker family.[6] Eldo, who had tried his hand at various jobs, at last settled down near North Vernon as a renter on some land now covered by the Jefferson Proving Ground; and he worked for his father-in-law as a day laborer. At the time, it seemed that he would stay as poor as his own family was; nor was it consolation enough for him to know that, in the histories of Jefferson County, his own forebears rather than his wife's had left their names on the land. To worsen matters, Grace was ailing in health.

On July 18, 1902, their first child was born, Mary Jessamyn; and between her and the poetry-reciting, bookish grandmother a mutual affection soon blossomed. No doubt Grandmother Milhous proved to be an important intellectual as well as emotional stimulant for the young Jessamyn. Within a very few years Myron and Carmen were born, and the latter seems to have been the model for Blix in *A Matter of Time*.

Year after year the treadmill of farm work turned; but, meanwhile, Uncle Frank Milhous invested in California real estate and moved his own family to the Quaker community of Whittier, which was named for the Quaker poet. Fortunately for Eldo, whose proximity to the Milhous family must have irked him, an excellent opportunity arose. Grace's father had been one of those interested enough in Los Angeles land investment to buy an orange grove, one that some years later yielded a high income when duly subdivided into building lots. Such speculations were a sign of the new materialism rapidly entering into the lives of the erstwhile simple Friends almost everywhere, a materialism to be lamented in *A Matter of Time*. This orange grove Eldo was to manage temporarily until he had time to make his own investment. The change from Indiana to the sunshine of California was beneficial to Grace's health, and the move meant a new start for them in a lonely and somewhat rugged last frontier.

II *In the Sun That Is Young Once Only*

Grandmother Milhous wanted to keep Mary Jessamyn in Indiana because she feared there would be insufficient intellectual stimulation on the frontier for such a lively girl; nevertheless, the parents insisted on taking her with them as they left for California on the train on a rainy April day in 1909. The grandmother, until her death three years later, saw that her hazel-eyed, befreckled, tow-headed favorite received packages of books, magazines, and hand-decorated dresses.[7] After reaching the "Golden state," the Wests lived for two years in a bungalow in the orange grove at East Whittier. Although surrounded by relatives on neighboring ranches, Mrs. West soon became lonely for Indiana and began to tell the children stories of the "good old days" back East.

Mr. West eventually bought some wilderness land in the Yorba Linda tract in Orange County and planted a lemon grove.[8] They roughed it in a tent at Yorba Linda for a while, then moved into an unpainted house that Mr. West had constructed on a windy hilltop at the edge of "town" north of Club Terrace and Yorba Linda Boulevard.[9] The frail mother, troubled with caring for three small children, and later a fourth, was doubtless grateful to get away from the crawling rattlers outdoors; but the centipedes had a way of sneaking in through cracks.

In his planting of lemons, West correctly anticipated the drift of agriculture toward citrus fruits; for, by 1916, three-fourths of the original tract was in oranges and lemons,[10] a promising business in view of the soil, the warm climate, and the recently incorporated Yorba Linda Water Company[11] that soon provided irrigation. Yorba Linda lay bare in the sun on the rim of what used to be the great arid, sandy wastes jutting up through south-central California until, just after the turn of the century, the railroad and, more especially, irrigation fostered an agricultural revolution for much of the state. Jessamyn grew up in a region increasingly domesticated with fruit orchards and not many miles away from truck gardens and grain ranches.

Since the Yorba Linda of her girlhood figures in three of her books —*Cress Delahanty, South of the Angels,* and *A Matter of Time*— a little more should be disclosed about this community. In the year of her arrival in California, the undulating sagebrush and brown hills of Yorba Linda contained only one house.[12] The tract was largely the home of the ground squirrel, of the trapdoor spider, and of weird rolling balls of sagebrush that tumbled along with the dry Santa Ana wind. Aloft, coasting buzzards peered down upon Saddle Back Mountain toward the east, cinnamon foothills toward the north, a forest of oil rigs at Olinda in the Chino Hills to the northwest, and just three miles south the glimmering curve of the Santa Ana River as it rolled to the Pacific.

To Jessamyn's eyes, when she first saw the area, all the "wild and spare and tawny" landscape was beautiful. In the spring, "Grass swept across the hillsides like green fire," she wrote feelingly in a hometown newspaper article in 1947. "Reservoir Hill was carpeted with yellow violets. . . .There were other flowers, of course, and on other hills. . . .Indian paint brushes, baby blue eyes, Mariposa lilies, lupine. In Yorba Linda in the early days no one had to wait for heaven to claim his bed of flowery ease," for every hillside had a floral blanket.[13] With the joyous insouciance of youth, she did not mind that the schoolhouse would not be ready on Olinda Street until the coming September, that the Santa Ana blew loose shingles from rooftops, that water had to be hauled in by wagon from Atwood until the pipes and pumps were ready, that not until 1912 was there a general merchandise store in town—let alone electricity. Photographs from that day show a horse-and-buggy town where the automobile was scarce upon the streets.

Mr. West quickly became influential through election to the board of trustees for the school and, soon afterward, to the office of secretary or president. Over the years he worked as postmaster, garage owner, water company superintendent, owner of a dry cleaning plant, and realtor.[14] He earned enough income to give his family ample comforts (Jessamyn had no lack of silk dresses, she reports) and to send three of the children to college.

To be sure, the girl Jessamyn was no angel, despite the relative strictness of her upbringing. But whether or not, while on the long rambles with brother Myron through the hills, she "borrowed" fruit from the farms, as the neighborly Huckleberry Finn did, is not known. Since swimming was a forbidden but enticing luxury in such a warm climate, she joined other urchins in plunging into the irrigation canal when adults were not around. Her children in *South of the Angels* take delight in this very peccadillo.

Mrs. Gladys Gauldin, a playmate of this period, remembers in detail one incident indicating how cruel Jessamyn could be at age thirteen to the submissive. Accompanying the slightly older Gladys home one day with her bucket full of strawberries intended for a strawberry shortcake, Jessamyn picked up a switch and switched the girl at intervals to force her to give her berries to eat. When the victim reached home, there were few berries left. The memory of this little tyranny gave the adult Jessamyn some insight into the "sickening pleasures of cruelty and of the temptation the submissive offer to the aggressor to see just how far his submissiveness will go."[15] So disgusted was she by this blemish in herself that she gives a similar flaw to her villain, Mrs. Prosper, her scapegoat in the story "A Little Collar for the Monkey."

Miss West dates her adult intellectual life from age twelve, when one summer evening she checked out John Fox's *The Trail of the Lonesome Pine* from among fifty works on the shelves of the newly opened "library" in the janitor's closet at school.[16] Thereafter, reading became a passion; for today she can remember no finer pleasure than that of walking back from the library, "book and magazine laden, in early autumn twilight, or under summer stars . . .with an evening's reading" in prospect. Her practice was to finish nightly one book and then begin another; in so doing, she felt stronger through her ability to finish the first, and she was assured of an abundant tomorrow by having a book already started.[17]

Thanks to the collection owned by Grandmother Milhous, she made inroads into the works of a fellow Hoosier, Gene Stratton-Porter, with whose literary technique and career she was to have a few striking resemblances. She waded into E. P. Roe, whose novels of sentimental piety gather dust today on library shelves. More meaty reading came with William Wordsworth, Edgar Allan Poe, Palgrave's *Golden Treasury*, *The Oxford Book of Victorian Poetry*, Thomas Carlyle's *Heroes and Hero Worship*, Hippolyte Taine's *History of English Literature*, Charles Dickens' *David Copperfield*, and the literature of Anton Chekhov, Hilaire Belloc, and G. B. Shaw. Her girlhood reading diet consisted mainly, however, of poetry and novels, as she admits; but there was also a generous helping of socialism 'a la Jane Addams and Jack London, a subject much favored then by *avant-garde* intelligentsia, that helped make her sympathetic toward downtrodden minority groups, such as the "greasers" (Mexican-Americans) in *South of the Angels.*

As expected of a Quaker girl, she had a taste for reading journals; but she was not restricted to those of George Fox, John Woolman, and their ilk; for instance, Samuel Pepys had a special appeal. What has seemed "uncanny" to her (using her own word) is that, long before she discovered she had tuberculosis, she was forcibly drawn to tubercular authors and those who wrote about the disease, whether in the form of journal or finished art: John Keats, Henry D. Thoreau, the Brontës, Katherine Mansfield, the already mentioned Chekhov, Marie Bashkirtsev, Thomas Mann (*Magic Mountain*), and no doubt others. Perhaps it is best to accept Miss West's own explanation that she was drawn to tubercular writers and journal-keepers because of "their ability to endure, their Stoicism." Her weakening health during her twenties may well have disposed her to seek out authors similarly handicapped who could, through the notable examples of their lives, offer implicit consolation. Mansfield, who allured her most strongly, early became her heroine, both as a fiction writer and as a personality: "There was a time when I didn't think I could start a day writing without reading some in her journal." But more must be said later about Thoreau, whose influence upon Jessamyn West is indelible.

To certain modern authors she has responded affectionately. Her fellow Californian William Saroyan is one who once had a slight (though unfortunate) influence upon her as a beginning writer, in that the opening story of *Friendly Persuasion* was originally entitled "No Uncle of Saroyan" and had in it several Saroyan references which were later wisely deleted.[18] But Saroyan also had a *useful* influence upon her, as we shall see later. Along with Mansfield, Virginia Woolf became a favorite with her. About the time her writing career began, Jessamyn West had already decided to become the Virginia Woolf of the 1940's,[19] an ambition soon enough fulfilled and even surpassed with respect to subtle literary technique, over-all quality, and intrinsically interesting story matter. The writings of Eudora Welty have from the beginning evoked in this Quaker woman of letters an almost boundless admiration.[20] Hemingway also became popular with her, as he did with so many beginning writers of her generation. However, none of the authors she encountered has ever been to Miss West a model for conscious imitation, although it is likely that from such figures as Mansfield and Woolf, maybe Welty—the possibilities are numerous and the influence difficult to trace—she derived some of her skill with modes of narration.

Jessamyn's brother, Merle, says that his sister made daily hoards of new words to improve her vocabulary,[21] a practice which Cress Delahanty used for her notebook of beautiful words and phrases. Nonetheless, this girlhood interest in vocabulary was not accompanied by any conscious effort at authorship; for it took many years to overcome her awe of literary people (great writers seemed like magicians) so that she could dare to compose a story. As additional but unwitting preparations for authorship, she began at some time to keep a journal, forty volumes of which have accumulated,[22] as well as a few writing notebooks.

III *School Days: Playing in Many Keys*

In due time, Miss West began to commute to Fullerton Union High School which shared a campus with the affiliated Fullerton Junior College. In high school she took the usual subjects, including Latin.[23] Her grades, as Merle affirms, were far above average; one report card shows a predominance of B+'s and A's. Her English compositions were so outstanding that the faculty sent her to read them to other classes.[24] Among various extracurricular activities, she edited *The New Pleiades* (a weekly published jointly by the two schools).

Here, and later in the junior college, the students in organized forensics found they had an able new voice among them. Indeed, a notice in the school paper records that "Jessyman" West and Flora Walker roundly defeated the Santa Ana Junior College team.[25] The debating coach and college director, Dr. William T. Boyce, taught her a course in the then new subject of economics. From all the evidence, Dr. Boyce seems to have been one of those rare teachers who so encourage and inspire their students as to live on in their minds and hearts—and thereby extend indefinitely their subtle influence. He was memorably impressed by Miss West: "Her face, then as now, lights up showing interest, enthusiasm. . . .There was no monotony in the flow of words. She played on many keys. She had a fine sense of humor and in a debate used it sparingly but with expressive results. The use of her hands was as natural as was her voice."[26]

Incidentally, several of Miss West's acquaintances have remarked that she speaks rapidly; a crude stanza about her in *The Pleiades* (high school yearbook) tends to confirm this fact.[27] Her mature speech, however, is known to be precise, clear, intense, and animated, as the present writer can well confirm on the basis of conversations with her. Boyce, in the foregoing letter, remembers that she made friends easily but seemed to have no "bosom pals." She revealed, he also remembers, a strain of unconventionality by bobbing her hair when this style was not yet acceptable. He recalls a delightful, unforgettable girl who was generally "at loose-ends with books, sweaters, rain togs. . . . Her mind was too occupied with her many facets of interest and responsibility to keep track of her belongings."

A schoolmate from the Whittier period recollected that Jessamyn wore "a very stern look," yet smiled readily, enjoyed being around other students, and was lively in a group.[28] Various reports from contemporaries paint the over-all image of a happy if somewhat reserved and serious schoolgirl who was eager for knowledge and experience; if anything, she was the superabundantly normal intellectual trying on her first blue stockings. A photograph of her in *The Pleiades* shows a smiling, impish face, full of joyous self-possession and animal spirits.

In the fall after high school graduation, Jessamyn matriculated at the then sectarian Whittier College which had been founded by the Society of Friends in 1901. She arrived a little late, in 1919, to be a student under the future playwright Maxwell Anderson, who had taught there a year as a professor of English before being discharged for, of all things, pacifist convictions. A little after Miss West's time, the novelist Dorothy Baker attended the school, and still later Richard M. Nixon (one of his cousin's devoted readers). As a freshman who was still aglow from her triumphs at Fullerton, Jessamyn had difficulties with a beautiful composition teacher, a "tall Rossetti-like woman" who later, it is said, suffered a mental breakdown. This redheaded creature disliked one of Jessamyn's themes entitled "Braided Eye Beams," which was based upon her own discovery of the twisted eye beams motif used so memorably by John Donne in a poem. After class, the teacher told the girl to curb her imagination.

25

The theme that caused Jessamyn the most difficulty was entitled "Live Life Deeply." The outraged teacher copied the theme onto the blackboards for the class to see and spent the rest of the period demonstrating the author's moral and intellectual shortcomings. Jessamyn was so profoundly shocked and humiliated by this woman that she set out the next morning, dressed in white as befitted a sacrificial maiden, to drown herself. Providentially, the reservoir chosen was boarded over; therefore, she decided to have a bit of breakfast and then try again. But breakfast raised the would-be suicide's spirits so much that she postponed her attempt—and followed with other postponements.[29] The short story "Live Life Deeply" treats the attempted suicide in a somewhat fictionalized manner.

The negative influence of this English teacher was surely one of the factors that caused Miss West to delay until her late thirties the writing of stories. Notwithstanding the fact that her writing style early in college seems to have been studded with precious diction as the result of treasure hunts in the dictionary, any normal composition teacher ought to have been pleased with the prospect of having such brilliant talent to guide and improve. The opening of one of her college themes written at age seventeen has been published; it is a dazzling exercise in the use of recherché words beginning with the letter "a."[30]

For various reasons—including dating for the first time and her matrimonial engagement to be married by the end of the freshman year—living life *too* deeply?—her grade average plummeted.[31] Thereupon she transferred to the junior college where she came under the stimulus of Director Boyce, raised her grades, and played basketball. Back at Whittier in the fall of 1921, she earned a series of A's in literature and in other subjects on her way to her bachelor's degree in English. Somewhere in all this collegiate experience there must have been an old spinster who taught a nominally informative course in sex education, "Hygiene" as it is dubbed in the slightly fictionalized story "Love." In that story the spinster warns the all-girl class that boys are "different" from them, that "if a boy attempts to embrace you, draw away from him gently but firmly and say 'Think of your future children.' "[32] This prissy Victorianism was then prevalent almost everywhere in small American schools. The remarkable thing about Jessamyn West is that, with such a tradition to build upon—or, rather, deviate from—she even bothered to write at all; the odds against her becoming a realistic author who tried to express the truth about the sexes must have been tremendous. In the true biographies of most famous people, *despite* probably occurs as often as *because of*.

In her senior year, Miss West took sociology from a superb young teacher, Paul S. Smith, who later became the president of the college; and she made a vivid impression on him as a vivacious and apt scholar.[33] Surviving is a paper she did for her class about a sociological trip to the courts of Los Angeles. Though rife with errors of punctuation and spelling, the style is crisp in its use of antithesis, irony, wide vocabulary, and occasional exclamatory phrases; the diction is not at all precious. The evaluations she made are seemingly based on objective evidence and proposed with an awareness of the difficulties of studying social phenomena. Suffusing the whole is a sense of humaneness and justice, despite the obvious desire to be "scientific." The paper has no literary merit, obviously enough; but it is interesting as an early example of the firsthand observation which Jessamyn had to practice, consciously or otherwise, to become a creative writer.[34]

Although no dancing or card playing was permitted at Whittier, Jessamyn seems to have had an agreeable time. Evidently, she continued to indulge her love of reading. As at Fullerton, she plunged into a variety of extracurricular activities, including holding offices in the Palmer Literary Society. Her dramatic interest, manifest in the high school years, extended to acting in some skits and in the senior class play.[35]

IV *Crisis*

The youth to whom Miss West had become engaged in her freshman year was Harry Maxwell McPherson, the son of a Quaker family in Whittier. On August 16, 1923, two months after her graduation, they were married in the Yorba Linda Friends Church.[36] From a miscellany of sources, we may reliably reconstruct the events of the next few years during which the McPhersons moved about a good deal. McPherson himself was blessed with continual offers of better jobs; but he ultimately returned to finish college, earn a doctorate in education, and rise through various high school principalships to become the superintendent of schools at Napa. At present, he teaches at the University of California.

In 1924, Miss West and her husband went to live in his parents' apricot orchard at Hemet. At first, she worked as a school secretary; but she soon began four years of teaching in a clock-less, plumbing-less, one-room school a few miles from the ranch. She gives us a view of a school very much like it in the opening paragraph of "The Singing Lesson" in *Love Death and the Ladies' Drill Team*: "Liberty School is built on a piece of low, unusable alkaline land. There are no other buildings in sight. In spring it rises like a lighthouse above great fields of ripening barley; in fall its shadow is long morning and evening across far-reaching stretches of stubble. In winter it stands solitary in the center of a pool of shallow, wind-scalloped water" (234).

In this little, isolated building she taught all six grades; and, surprisingly enough, she loved the work. Despite the demanding routine, she must have had her daydreams, too, wondering when she would find time and sufficient excuse to write her books. The wind blowing about the schoolhouse in the forementioned story is made to speak to the teacher, significantly named Miss Mary McManaman: "It said far. It said distant, strange, remote. It said someday."

Even if Miss West had never read or were never to read any of the Katherine Mansfield stories about children, this experience in the school would have furnished her with numerous observations for stories and novels about young people. Hardly any student of human nature can read "The Singing Lesson" without feeling that Miss West is a person who would establish excellent rapport with children. As a matter of fact, one of her friends, Mr. Richard Scowcroft of Stanford University, confirms this ability, adding that she speaks to them with directness and interest, never condescendingly.[37] During the 1950's the McPhersons' affection for teen-agers found outlet in taking a lad named Fred Oswald as a ward into the Napa household for three years,[38] and later the sisters Ann and Jean McCarthy direct from Limerick, Ireland, joined their family. An international affair preluded the rearing of the McCarthy girls. Unlike the church authorities in Dublin, the San Francisco archbishop would not approve of Catholics entering a Quaker household; and it required the intercession of Miss West's cousin, who then was Vice-President Nixon of the United States, to convince the American archbishop through others in Dublin that the McPhersons did not intend to tamper with the girls' religion.[39]

Because the career of a college professor with a doctorate in English began to appeal to her, Miss West resigned from her teaching post to attend graduate school. In the summer of 1929 she was studying at Oxford University; however, the lure of Old World sights proved stronger than that of the lecture hall. After the summer session ended, she traveled to Paris, the first of at least six trips to the Continent that she was to make over the years.[40] In midwinter, she joined her husband at the University of California, at Berkeley, for a year and a half of study.

Although the rigors of the doctoral program did not prevent her making rapid progress, she soon saw that studying was another postponement of her dream. From the age of twelve, she had kept some notebooks of story ideas for use someday; but when would she ever use them? One of her letters underscores the sense of failure: "I can remember (here in Berkeley, from where I write) getting up from my study table, going to a rain drenched window, to look out, I thought, and to review in my mind the French I had just memorized; and instead to weep and say, 'When am I ever going to write my stories?' "[41]

To this frustration there would soon be added another far more serious difficulty, which to the latent artist needing some good excuse to write—and Jessamyn West sorely needed an excuse—would come as a blessing terrible as the storied monkey's paw. She had barely reached her twenty-ninth birthday when the date was set for her doctoral orals, but the sudden illness of one of the examining professors caused the date to be postponed, whereupon she and her husband visited her parents' home. There, jumping from bed one morning, as Katherine Mansfield had done before her, she tasted a warm-salty gush of arterial blood in her mouth—a tubercular hemorrhage. Within three days she entered La Viña Sanitorium near Pasadena, for X-rays had revealed a far-advanced case wherein both lungs were equally affected.[42] The patient-physician relationship is reflected in the story "The Condemned Librarian," published in *Crimson Ramblers of the World, Farewell.*

Considering her condition, her survival was almost a miracle; for only 5 percent of the "far advanced" cases admitted to tuberculosis sanitoriums were alive after five years.[43] Nine anxious months followed in those frame buildings on the mountainside before Jessamyn West at last went home to Yuba City where her husband lived; but only a few weeks later the tuberculosis flared again, and she was brought back to La Viña on a stretcher. Not long afterward, the doctor told her parents that nothing more could be done; she might as well be taken home to die in the company of loved ones.[44]

V *Horizontal Life*

And so Miss West went to live in her parents' home where Grace West would tolerate no nonsense about dying. A period of long couch or bed life began that did not end until 1945. Under her mother's care, she began to improve. Had Grace West not been the emotionally vital person she was—"a life-enhancer if there ever was one"[45]—her daughter might not have survived to write a single story.

Grace West, who clearly influenced the daughter and her books, was a woman of delightful contradictions. Shy and retiring by habit, she was also capable of vigorous expressiveness on some occasions as well as of unexpected prankishness. The repressive, backwoods Quaker in her, partly due to a tradition of numerous preachers in the family, produced a sex fear in her concerning her children; and this overprotectiveness may be seen in Lib of *The Witch Diggers*. Yet the lively McManamans and Sharps in her blood, the family strain of which Jessamyn West inherited full measure, were constantly rubbing against the staid, conventional Milhouses. The Elfin side sometimes dominated her actions, as when Grace, bored at a Girls' League party in Jessamyn's high school gymnasium, seized a dangling rope and swung from the balcony over the heads of the startled females.[46] Extant is a copy of a hilarious burlesque letter that she reportedly sent to one of Jessamyn's former professors at Whittier; unhappily, space does not permit its inclusion.[47]

Within half a year, Miss West sufficiently recovered to rejoin her husband, then employed in Yuba City; and a photograph of her from this time shows a woman sadly altered from the college days; she looks pathetically ill, seemingly middle-aged already, and much overweight from tubercular fat. With much leisure on her hands, Jessamyn West once more turned to reading books. On one of these occasions she chanced upon a story by William Saroyan, likewise a member of a minority group, whose expressed belief is that all one needs to do to compose a story is to ignore the rules of other people, forget how such-and-such a famous author wrote, never try to arrive at style, write voluminously without regard to care, and learn to typewrite. But what Miss West found in the Saroyan story as representing maximum requirements, "a lot of feeling and a free-flowing pen," emboldened her to break down a psychological impediment and to construct her first story "99.6" about sanitorium life.[48]

Some of the published biographical articles, as well as communications from her acquaintances, might delude us into thinking that her first stories originated during the months in the sanitorium, even *The Friendly Persuasion!*; but she was actually too ill either for serious writing or for reading. The conscious and formal work had to wait at least two years; for not until out of the sanitorium and while still flat on her back and unable to do anything else did she feel it would not be presumptuous—no visible "call" in evidence upon her, no excuse for putting off any more the act of writing—for her to begin to write. The extended illness, having forbidden so many of her usual activities, gave her the solitude and the leisure with which to expand her notebook writing into more or less finished "pieces." In depriving her of so much else, tuberculosis forced her to accept as real and valuable her literary imagination.[49]

In the story "Home-Coming," which deals with the tuberculosis experience, she insinuates that an organism under germ attack strives harder than ever at reproduction; just so, by analogy or sublimation (or both), her artistic psyche rose at what seemed the eleventh hour and defied death in expressing at long last its own peculiar form of fertility. Doubtless, the realization of her dream now gave her something of urgent importance for which to live. Possibly in this period of culmination of a long frustrated desire began what Miss West prefers to describe as "that continuous elation which is the chief fact of my life."[50]

Although this tubercular experience was to influence her writings —as is shown later—and to restrict them in significant ways, it did not make them pallid, squeamish, or preoccupied very long with disease or death. Probably the most striking and memorable result of the tuberculosis calamity, aside from shoving a wistful, five-foot-seven-inch-tall scribbler of journals into writing literature, is something on the order of an esthetic revelation in several of her best works: a preternatural awakening to the wonder of being alive and alert to all the senses, to a glory enwrapping even common things. On the other hand, perhaps an already existing sensibility was merely revived or encouraged to thrive. The spiritual renewal at the end of Edna St. Vincent Millay's "Renascence" describes this change admirably.

According to Miss West's article which she prepared exclusively for "Grandma" Sue Lucas' "On the River" column of March 5, 1970, in *The Parker Pioneer* (Parker, Arizona), she had at first refused to mail any stories to possible publishers until her husband's chidings became unbearable. To satisfy him, she consented to send a dozen to as many magazines on condition that he cease talking about publication if they were all rejected. Fortunately, "about the third" story was accepted.

VI *Fulfillment*

Consequently, unlike many celebrated writers, Miss West broke into print without any difficulty and any heartbreaks. She sent most of her early work to nonpaying magazines and thus unwittingly spared herself the minuscule payments that so embarrass ambitious beginners. Not at all dependent upon writing for pecuniary support, she could well afford to forego such embarrassment. Even so, she has always been humble and unassuming in her dealings with editors, a behavior quaintly out of keeping with what we might expect from so gifted an artist. She admits profiting from and being grateful for the critical comments of some editors; and among these were Dudley Wynn (*New Mexico Quarterly*), Mary Louise Aswell (*Harper's Bazaar*), Edward Weeks (*Atlantic*), Katherine White (*New Yorker*), Kay Gauss Jackson (*Harper's Magazine*), Hugh Kahler (*Ladies' Home Journal*), and Lowry C. Wimberly (*Prairie Schooner*).[51]

The hesitant author kept "99.6" from the market for years, but it won a prize when published in *Broun's Nutmeg* in June, 1939. That summer the story "Homecoming," also about sanitorium life, won no prize in *American Prefaces*; but it is clearly a much better work. Having cured herself of the tuberculosis motif, she quickly turned to various other subjects, in keeping with a healthy artistic development. She retained California as a favorite fictional locale and added to it southern Indiana. In the fall of 1939, *Foothills* carried "The Day of the Hawk," a psychological study of a neurotic woman whose sense of guilt over her infant's death eventually becomes an Albert Schweitzer "reverence for life." Not too surprising, the narrator is a convalescing female who lives in Yorba Linda and who has a whole row of personal journals to her credit. The story is cleverly done, although the dialogue (as reported from a journal) sounds strained in places.

Her first publishing year is interesting for at least three reasons. First, she began quite early to draw upon her own experience as a girl and young lady in Southern California for stories. Her life was to be for her the stuff of which books are made, but not in the intensely autobiographical fashion of Thomas Wolfe. She is far too imaginative to be content with a slight juggling of personal "facts" or, except with *A Matter of Time*, with a disguising of real-life persons. As George Washington Cable had said that the best stories rest somewhere upon a factual basis, Jessamyn West founded some, but by no means all, of her best work on a little isle of fact amid a great big sea of fancy, making use of identifiable personal experience and family tradition. Second, her interest in juvenile figures, finally leading to some of her most popular books, found expression in "The Mush Pot," later cast into a *Cress Delahanty* story. And, third, her interest in back-country, Indiana life gave rise to the first of the *Friendly Persuasion* stories, "Music on the Muscatatuck." Exceedingly early in her career, then, she began using characters and locales that became prominent in subsequent books. The important themes, nonetheless, emerge but gradually, save for the tubercular one enunciated in the beginning and thereafter recurring occasionally.

Late in 1945, Harcourt, Brace published *The Friendly Persuasion*, a unified collection of narratives about the Quaker couple Jess and Eliza Birdwell. Almost overnight Jessamyn West was famous. From now on there would be no more "horizontal life" for her; instead, an active career of writing, traveling, and teaching began.

During Mrs. West's final illness, following a series of strokes that left her unable to recall the identities of her children, she once revealed a well-kept secret that fairly startled her fictionist-daughter. In recalling to her who she was, Miss West said she was that woman who wrote the Quaker stories. " 'Oh Jessamyn,' " the mother misunderstood, " '*did* I get them written? I was always going to write from the time I was a girl. . . .' " And the daughter recovered quickly enough to answer: "Yes you did, Mama. You got them all written. There's a whole book of them . . . everything you ever thought about the Quakers and the old days in Indiana is down in print."[52]

Still, we must be careful not to accept always the mother at the daughter's grateful valuation. That she stimulated her daughter's imagination goes without saying; that she furnished some germs for stories is no doubt true; however, Miss West performed all that vital, prolonged labor and had the necessary imagination which makes the difference between exhilarating and even provocative reportage and the sometimes stunning artistic creation.

A *Mirror for the Sky* (1948) represented her first and last attempt at operetta. She seems to have perceived fairly early where her forte lay: short stories and novels. The first of the novels, *The Witch Diggers* (1951), had a Hoosier setting around the turn of the century. In succeeding novels and unified story collections, she moved forward chronologically, passing from the parental into personal recollections. The time and setting of *Cress Delahanty* (1953) is approximately that of Miss West's own childhood in Yorba Linda. In *Love Death and the Ladies' Drill Team* (1955), Miss West collected many of the better short stories printed earlier in "little magazines" and in *Harper's*, the *New Yorker*, and the *Saturday Evening Post*.

To See the Dream (1957) has that garrulous, comfortable air of an author assured of her audience. Ostensibly transcribed from her hitherto unpublished journals, it is the only extended piece of autobiography yet to come from Miss West. In 1959 appeared the philosophical essay *Love Is Not What You Think*.

Her second novel was somehow delayed until 1960, partly because of its unusual length. Also, traveling about on speaking engagements, receiving honorary doctorates (from Whittier, Mills, Swarthmore, Indiana University, Western College for Women), attending writer's conferences, and teaching creative writing at universities seriously interfered with composition. "Talking," she declares ruefully, "is the death of writing."[53] The novel *South of the Angels* proved her capable of structural complexity in handling a whole community of fictional families on a tract near Whittier. Later, her scholarly training was used in editing an extensively annotated anthology of Quaker writings, *The Quaker Reader* (1962), which Perry Miller favorably reviewed.[54]

A Matter of Time (1966), the third novel, brought her finally to the present-day setting, thereby marking a radical departure for her. Next year the fourth novel, *Leafy Rivers*, appeared. Early 1969 saw the publication of the best seller *Except for Me and Thee*, which consisted of additional Jess Birdwell stories that round out the scheme of *Friendly Persuasion*. In September, 1970, came her second collection of miscellaneous stories, under the colorful title of *Crimson Ramblers of the World, Farewell*. One project awaiting publication is an edited anthology of John J. Audubon's writings;[55] another project, now underway, is a book of nonfiction tentatively called *Walden on Wheels*.

VII   *The Author at Work*

Motion-picture scriptwriting also lured her. She received sole credit for the script *Stolen Hours*; partial credit for *The Big Country*; but no credit at all for *Friendly Persuasion*, despite her collaboration, because the studio wanted to avoid legal difficulties with the Screen Writers Guild.[56] Although Miss West resents the corporate method of originating scripts, one indigenous to Hollywood, she still welcomes the challenges of the film medium. If this satisfaction were not enough, the money from the sale of motion-picture rights ought to have pleased her. *Friendly Persuasion* earned a modest fortune,[57] and *South of the Angels*, sold to Metro Goldwyn-Mayer, was still more lucrative.

Contrary to the common experience of the fiction writer who goes to Hollywood, where the average film director is rumored to be a tasteless Mephistophelian peddler of dreams, Miss West claims substantial advantages from her stints there. More is said in later chapters about the Hollywood influence.

She practices her craft as soon as possible after breakfast each day in Napa, lying on or in her bed as Twain did, or in an attic study, or in a bedroom study in the barn, or even outdoors by the swimming pool while seated in a reclining chair with a clipboard in her lap.[58] Recently, she has sought refuge from visitors and autograph seekers by doing her writing in a house trailer parked along the river near Parker, Arizona. Writing while lying down or reclining is a habit she acquired from the sanatorium episode. The handwritten manuscripts are all made with a fountain pen in a surprisingly legible script upon yellow legal pads (8-1/2″ x 14″). At the time this study is being written, the practice is to have a housewife acquaintance type up three or four copies of a given work before the final version is reached.

There is very little outlining. Miss West puts into the initial attempt the best effort she can command at the time, *as if* that might result in the first and final draft, even though the first draft commonly turns out to be exceedingly rough and needs many revisions. The general method, including the omission of the outline, suggests the "organic theory" of art wherein the story assumes its own form, in conformity with some interior 'necessity or other, independent of any preconceived design on the part of the artist. Counterpointing this "organic" method, however, is the conscious and (we must assume) planned revision—for even such famous exponents of the method as R. W. Emerson and Walt Whitman had their judicious afterthoughts, as attested by altered manuscripts and textual variants.[59]

One reason Miss West does so little outlining, it may well be, is to insure spontaneity in the product and the impression of immediacy born of recent discovery. The act of writing is to her in the nature of a fresh adventure, not the keeping of a tightly scheduled appointment: "Some writers have their stories so carefully planned that they never change a word once it is on paper. Some writers keep elaborate notebooks and files of ideas. I have no files or real story notebooks [she evidently excepts the notebooks from childhood], but I do rewrite many times. I rewrite not only to get a sentence to suit me, but because I do not know all of my story until I have written it." Furthermore, "I expect my characters to reveal more of themselves to me as the story progresses. I think the writer, as well as the reader, deserves a few surprises in the story."[60]

The implication of these statements is that a certain character might undergo in the art of origination a good deal of unforeseen development; then she must make such changes to prepare for the twists of plot necessitated by the new characterization. In an interview reported in the May, 1967, issue of *Writer's Digest*, Miss West admits that what comes first to her mind is "the person in a situation"—not any thing to prove and not any complete plot—after which she learns about the story as she writes.

Her stories apparently do take form in this way. But a writer's explanation of his technique, as with Edgar A. Poe's composing "The Raven," need not necessarily be complete. Even geniuses have never satisfactorily explained genius. Nor does it follow that the method used with one work applies to others by the same author. Nonetheless, the following description of her method is applicable to at least one of her stories; and it reveals that the chief characters were formed early before the story was clear.

In a letter she writes that "things as they actually happen rarely make good stories. . . . There's no satisfaction in 'repeating'—only in creating."[61] What matters is the tiny bud of suggestion that alights like yeast in the imagination and works away until wine develops. In "The Story of a Story" she describes in gripping detail how her account of the schizoid physician, Dr. Chooney, pullulated. First, she saw on a driving trip a large, isolated, mysterious house with a physiotherapist's sign posted by the highway. In this instance, the locale or setting preceded both character and plot in the story that would ultimately coalesce. The remote and run-down situation of the house caused her to speculate upon its occupant. Immediately, Gothic overtones arose; for these are discernible in the significant questions she asked herself about the house. And, in explanation of the questions, she states that "There is a self beneath the surface who knows all the answers—to the right questions." And she sounds almost like a Transcendentalist when, affirming the value of intuition, she adds: "One must be careful only to ask the right question, to ask it in a low voice, and to wait."[62] Again the organic principle is apparent; the given story situation will naturally give rise to its own proper actors and actions if the writer ponders significant questions and waits. In this instance, Miss West waited six months—but, meanwhile, she was working on other stories—until she had a name for the doctor (later changed), gave him a daughter (later changed to a patient-victim), and knew that he was somehow evil.

Other significant questions were posed; then there was another six months of waiting. Meanwhile, she heard from her housekeeper a certain anecdote that somehow appealed to the unconscious part of herself as a storyteller; she luckily set down this anecdote in her journal. In due time, she discovered that what she had recorded was the answer for which she had been looking. Three years after first sighting the house she began "Horace Chooney, M.D."

This history of creation is the only detailed one that Miss West has given thus far about any of her fiction. For two reasons, the foregoing explanation is not to be taken as typical of her procedure: (1) Her stories are in practically every instance constructed much, much faster than was this one. (2) "Horace Chooney, M.D." is one of a very few in the West corpus having, as she says, a "considerable basis in the external world." As a rule, she shies away from the ready-made story handed her by someone else; she prefers the glittering fragment upon which the imagination can play and envision the whole. We can be sure she eschews—and gladly—the reportorial technique that Stephen Crane plied in "The Open Boat": manipulating an actual incident, replete with most details intact, from the life experience of the author.

In critical theory, Miss West agrees with V. S. Pritchett that what a writer is striving to do is to learn his own identity; and he does so by removing as many of the veils as possible that hide him from himself.[63] Jessamyn West posits in "The Story of a Story" that the artist searching for his private identity "assumes in turn the identities of as many of his fellow men as the breadth of his genius permits. In his search for himself he discovers us." This Romantic idea also has its parallel in "The American Scholar" of Emerson, whom she read early: "He then learns that in going down into the secrets of his own mind he has descended into the secrets of all minds. He learns that he who has mastered any law in his private thoughts, is master to that extent of all men whose language he speaks, and of all into whose language his own can be translated."

Accordingly, in the chambers of the novelist's heart she throws back the draperies to disclose the sadistic and selfish Mrs. Prosper—for at some point while writing "A Little Collar for the Monkey" she must have known what it was like to be Mrs. Prosper and the other figures too. And so it must have been also for proud Lib Conboy of *Witch Diggers*, and the lonely Asa Brice of *South of the Angels*, and even the lustful Tom Mount from this same last novel. The writer, being a microcosm of all sins and virtues, suffers or rejoices, as the case may be, with his successive characters; but he does so, not because the characters are projections grounded outside himself and subject to his passing expressions of feeling, but because they are mirror images of his own secret self, of what he has been, or of what he might still become. The literary theory implies an Aristotelian purging of the emotions (for the artist, at least) by means of psychotherapy.

With such a theory, Jessamyn West should and does lean toward Realism, her own life being the principal quarry out of which she carves her literary valuables. Even the two science-fiction stories "The Pismire Plan" (1948) and "Little Men" (1954)—retitled *The Chilekings* (1967)—use her native Southern California as the locale. She reminds us, in some ways, of the practice of Jack London—whose famous ranch is near Napa, and who was at the apogee of his fame when she first entered the state—not only in the frequent reference to scenes of their youth before early sickness struck West and London in their late twenties and early thirties, respectively, but also in the repeated glorification of ranch life in California as it existed for them during an identical period. There is something, too, of the pioneer spirit common, as *South of the Angels* bears witness, to the best work of Willa Cather. The Realism of Miss West includes not only fidelity to physical detail and historical accuracy but to human psychology in the tradition of Henry James, whose critical observations she had read approvingly by 1949. She shares James's interest in fine consciences and in stylistic subtleties, but she never carries the cerebral distinctions and meanderings so far as to betray her into tedium.[64]

Some of her writing that contains lusty bed scenes is in keeping with Naturalism. One of the most noticeable features of all, yet the one least likely to be valued by Miss West herself, is the element of Romanticism that is evidenced by a recurring concern with the past; scenes of childhood and puberty; overweening preference for the rural over the urban; Thoreaulike sensitivity to the beauties of external nature; an inclination toward the grotesque and bizarre (*The Witch Diggers*) that is true of another 1951 novel by another American woman writer, Carson McCullers (*The Ballad of the Sad Cafe*); emphasis on the highly imaginative (science-fiction genre); and a fondness in some of her books for the remote or far away, specifically for the ancestral homesteads about North Vernon, Indiana, that was to her an alien country until she went there after finishing her first book.

CHAPTER 2

Olden Days Back "East"

I *Along The Muscatatuck*

MUCH of Jessamyn West's better writing ignores the ugliness and artificiality of mid-twentieth-century urban life and ensconces itself amid the bucolic back country America of previous eras. Her personal love for solitude as a housewife among her chores; her unusual predilection for the writings of Thoreau; her girlhood spent on ranches without (it seems) any important regrets; her dislike of, or at least uneasiness with, highway commercialism— all are consistent with the withdrawal and the idyllic tone found in *The Friendly Persuasion, A Mirror for the Sky, The Witch Diggers,* and *Leafy Rivers.* Early she discovered that, by retreating to a usable pattern of society already securely established in the past, she could avoid the pain of dealing in a literary way with her own unfortunate condition. Of course, the accessibility of bits of story material traditional in her family made it most convenient for her to use the Indiana past for several of her books.

Some unsuspecting readers of *The Friendly Persuasion* perhaps imagine its author as a little lady of church-mouse meekness attired in gray bonnet and First Day shawl, and as loyal as a Daughters of the American Revolution matron to her ancestral township of North Vernon, near which music-loving Jess Birdwell enacts his episodes. All these interpretations are essentially untrue, even though Miss West indubitably has tender feelings for various people in and about North Vernon, a place which she revisited as an adult, not only at the time of publication of *The Friendly Persuasion* but while working on *The Witch Diggers.*[1]

"I was tremulous about Southern Indiana for two reasons," she confides in a letter. "It was the fatherland . . . And it was the place I really knew nothing about, yet had written about. It was like— going back there that first time [1945], having staked your existence on the truth of a dream. . . ."[2] Most certainly this return was a pleasant one, for she was en route to New York to be honored at a reception by publishers who were bringing out her first book. Later, while constructing *The Witch Diggers*, she returned for a much longer sojourn to check on some nature descriptions she needed. At the railroad station she asked a porter whether she could take a taxi to the hotel. " 'Lady, if you take a taxi,' the porter replied, 'you're gonna plumb overshoot the town.' "[3] The porter did not exaggerate much, for North Vernon, although having been over many generations the railroad and highway center for Jennings County, had at the end of World War II fewer than thirty-five hundred residents, while the much older community of Vernon across the Muscatatuck had less than a tenth of that number. Confronting the visitor was a plain country hamlet, but one not so plain that beautiful souls could not dwell there, at least in imagination. Moreover, it was undeniably provincial, as is to be expected of isolated Midwestern communities of this size, but it was really no more provincial than, in another way, the Beacon Hill district of Boston, or the canyon neighborhoods of New York City.

If Vernon, in particular, looked as if it had fallen upon neglected days, Miss West could reflect that here once lay the headquarters for General Lew Wallace of *Ben Hur* fame during Morgan's raid of 1863, the site of a station on the underground railroad (see West's "Neighbors"), a courthouse where Henry Ward Beecher once spoke, the home of the now deceased author Phyllis Jackson (*Victorian Cinderella*), and the Rush Branch Church District near which Joshua Milhous had his nursery. Various buildings still standing here and across the river may have reminded her of the flour and woolen mills, the saw mills, the quarries, and the pork-packing companies which enjoyed no little prosperity in the 1800's. Probably she knew that flatboats had once docked at the forks of the river on the east side of Vernon. She could find here a sense of history even though the present might not offer much to her purposes.

She tried the hotel briefly, then shifted her quarters to Mrs. Rosa Toole Gordon's roominghouse on 106 Jennings in North Vernon, where the Irish landlady fascinated her with her racy and verbally rich talk. Nevertheless, Miss West spent much of her time in her room upstairs wrestling with the novel and living on oranges, crackers, cheese, and milk, except when she strolled out for dinner in some restaurant.[4] The boarders thought her mysteriously aloof. This roominghouse yielded materials for at least two of her works. The drunken ex-jockey in *The Witch Diggers* is patterned after one of the boarders.[5] And the story "Breach of Promise" was inspired by these rooms.[6] But it was not the hamlet but the slightly rolling outskirts that provided Miss West with settings for *The Friendly Persuasion* and *The Witch Diggers*, companion pieces that are markedly different in approach.

II The Friendly Persuasion: *Book*

About 1939, when her first stories were being published in "little magazines," Miss West turned to a series containing the idealistic nurseryman Jess Millhouse. It was lucky for her that John Woodburn of Harcourt, Brace saw the possibility of preparing a Quaker collection and talked her into the idea.[7] Once convinced, she persisted in the plan. Therefore, her hopes were not even appreciably dampened when an editor of Doubleday in 1941 rejected outright the idea of a collection.[8] Not even Thomas Wolfe's editor, Edward Aswell of Harper & Brothers, could budge her, two years later or thereabouts, when he suggested assimilating into a novel some of the stories he had seen; for a novel was more salable for a new author than a collection would be. She thought such a conversion quite beyond her powers.[9] Besides, was she not already well assured the stories had sufficient merit as they stood?

There were some outcries against the book even before it reached the presses. A certain kinsman, who took offense at the frank language in the magazine versions of the stories—"pa," "ain't," "duck dung"—and who also thought the fictional Millhouse family (Milhous) seemed right out of the family album, indicated that the stories should be linguistically deodorized, scrubbed, and dressed in such proper attire as would befit a genteel family tradition. The relative even wrote to Grace West and to an English professor at Whittier urging them to use their influence in bowdlerizing the stories, as letters possessed by Miss West verify. Outraged at the attempted censorship, the more since it occurred behind her back, Jessamyn West pointedly signified that the characters were *her* fictions—and not family history either—by changing Millhouse into the now Birdwell family. Too, she proudly clung to the offending words.

When *The Friendly Persuasion* received a favorable acceptance, despite the retained "vulgarities," the relative then donned Quaker costume and gave readings from the book. The erstwhile Millhouses, who had become Birdwells, were now said to be Milhouses and members of the speaker's own family. According to Miss West herself, the kinsman's attitude stood for everything that had to be overcome in her life before it was possible to write honestly: in fact, it accounted somewhat for the long delay in at last getting started.[10] In brief, she would have to overcome the tendency to be nice or good at the expense of being truthful, to be pretty at the expense of being honest. There was always the family to think of, or the Joneses next door—a sure route to a writer's frustration.

Following many a migraine headache and the ever threatening return of tuberculosis if she overexerted herself amid the enthusiasm of invention, she at last made the Birdwell collection a published fact—the first edition appearing on November 8, 1945, under the imprint of Harcourt, Brace; and the book was issued by Hodder & Stoughton in England next year. Almost without exception, the reviews were favorable; in many instances, they were cordial and glowing. Nathan L. Rothman in *Saturday Review* admired the style: "Miss West," he said, "wields a prose of a most friendly persuasion. It is as soft and musical as the speech of her Quakers, as sensitive to every manifestation of nature as they. . . ." Nor did he fail to mention the "sly wit" hiding hither and yon in the stories, and the "many passages of simple loftiness. . . ."[11] The *New Mexico Quarterly*, in whose pages some of her early endeavors were first manifest, loyally championed its former contributor as a "finely original, sensitive talent" operating in this instance with undeniable charm. "The flavor of Quaker speech, the Quaker humor [she could have said that it is characteristically a gentle one] and balance and tolerance are in its every sentence," the reviewer Katherine Simons noted; "seldom does an author achieve such harmony of expression and subject matter."[12]

The reception that had a special significance for Jessamyn West was that of the Quaker press, which was not quite so friendly. True, Richmond P. Miller in the *Friends Intelligencer* had for the new work nothing but praise,[13] and the English journal the *Friend* carried a pleasant if brief notice.[14] But *Friends Journal* bore then and at the time of the motion picture some letters of adverse criticism. One 1956 letter accused the author of being "disrespectful" toward the Society of Friends by using the "commonest of words"[15]—amusingly ironic coming from a member of a religious group that has always advocated plain and forthright language proper to a common folk. Of course everyone knows that common folk never use "ain't"

and "pa"! It just so happens that Miss West's Quaker ancestors actually did employ such words.[16] Anyone refusing to admit such
vocabulary into period fiction is being overly fastidious and unre-
alistic, expecially today.

We should hasten to add that the reading Friends at large were
not so slow in endorsing the book, at least privately, when they rec-
ognized the book's genuine esthetic and moral value, thus evincing
surer taste than might be deduced from some of their press coverage. With hardly any doubt, there must have been many now
unidentified but articulate readers outside the faith who hinted to
the Quakers that Miss West's work was an authentic cultural docu-
ment.

Perhaps Miss West did not from the beginning plan any larger
pattern when she wrote the first of these stories; yet there is a slight
pattern in the book collection—familial, chronological, and thematic
—as the résumés of the separate pieces demonstrate. The narratives are all told from the point of view of some Birdwell figure. The
father Jess has seven stories, Eliza and her children Josh and Mattie
have two each, and the granddaughter Elspeth one. They follow a
rough chronology: the first one shows Jess as a young Quaker husband operating the Maple Grove Nursery on the banks of the Muscatatuck before the Civil War (about 1852), and the last one ends
with him at a brave eighty, rich in children and happiness. In between the stories, children are born, such as Stephen, Jane (first
mentioned in "The Illumination"), and Little Jess (first mentioned
in "The Buried Leaf"). At some unspecified time between the first
and second stories, the tiny daughter Sarah is born and dies after a
pathetically brief youth.

"Music on the Muscatatuck," earliest of the items published,
begins as sheer poetry and is superbly fashioned to introduce the
series.[17] Its rhythmical opening paragraph is also a model of condensation giving the setting, a clapboard house along the river; the main
figure in the series to follow, Jess; his ancestry, Irish; his religion,
Quaker; his reading matter, the works of William Penn, John Woolman, and George Fox; the two dominant esthetic tastes in the family, music (represented by the starling in the cage) and floral beauty;
and even a hint at his occupation. We are surprised to learn that he
has a good-looking Quaker minister for a wife, Eliza. Here, a dream
removed from the Midwest as depicted in literature by E. W. Howe
and Hamlin Garland, is a land of trout fishing, roses, and fruits;

45

for poverty and drabness, boredom and the misery of ice-clad winter, are as scarce as Egyptians in an Israeli heaven.

Jess loyally lives up to the spirit of his religion, but he finds that certain austerities practiced in it are in opposition with his humanness. The beauties of this world are too much with him. Still hungering for music during a train trip, he permits the organ salesman "Professor" Quigley to talk him into buying one. The conversation between Quigley and Jess is delightfully amusing; and, as usual, the author underplays the whole dialogue; she is wary of saying too much, of being sentimental, or of even passing judgment. Here is Quigley baiting his victim with lachrymal lures as he presents the virtues of the Payson and Clarke instrument:

"... The throat of an angel. It cries, it sighs, it sings. You can hear the voice of your lost child in it. Did you ever lose a child. Brother Birdwell?"

"No" said Jess shortly.

"You can hear the voice of your old mother calling to you from the further shore."

"Ma lives in Germantown," said Jess.[18]

The reader is satisfied by this stage that Quigley's foxiness carries no harm and that what he is beguiling Jess into buying is wanted and needed by the music-starved fellow in the first place; hence, the reader figuratively leans back in his Pullman seat and enjoys the folksy humor played out before him.

Later, back at the nursery, there are fewer laughs when Eliza refuses to permit the instrument in the house, believing it might seduce the family with its sensuous, ear-flattering charms. After all, there are the neighbors and the Grove Meeting to consider. (She acts as she does because of the historical Quaker's prejudice against music.) To appease her and to make a concession to appearances, Jess hauls the organ into the attic, to which heaven he and Mattie soon learn to repair whenever the secular spirit of song moves them. In the climax of the story the ministry and oversight committee calls unexpectedly, and embarrassed Jess is hard put to drown out his daughter's upstairs playing. Still, he tries hard by delivering for that purpose a long, extempore prayer before the assembled elders, his voice booming out at each fortissimo pause until Mattie has run through "The Old Musician and His Harp" five times. After the elders hobble out, impressed with this strange outburst of piety, there occurs a final touch of humor when Jess again hears the song resume from upstairs and unrepentantly taps out the beat with his foot. Although there is no emphasis on landscape (true of all of Jessamyn West's work), "Music on the Muscatatuck" is the kind of story of which Washington Irving might have approved; for it has the hallmark of the true stylist, charm, a quaint local color, and goodhearted drollery.

"Shivaree before Breakfast" gains effectiveness by being told from the point of view of the Birdwell boys Joshua and Labe, aged thirteen and ten, respectively. Like the other Quakers in the stories, they speak the now quaint "thees" and "thous" which, with occasional dialect words found in and out of the dialogue, lend to the book some of its realistic flavor. These boys set out on foot one morning to shivaree a neighbor, Old Alf, whom they suspect of having secretly married; for Labe had overheard the old man addressing in terms of endearment a certain Molly in the house. But no wife trips to the window, only the bachelor. Invited inside, they are surprised to learn that Old Alf, because of his loneliness, has simply invented an imaginary loved one so that he can talk to someone.

Joshua, older and more conventional than his little brother, though less sympathetically responsive, feels that here is something dreadfully amiss in the adult sphere; therefore, when he assails Old Alf with "Thee's crazy," he is unwittingly fighting back the recognition that adulthood, which he had hitherto admired as a phase in which one is "not being worried or scared anymore" and in which one has "everything neat and happy," can, like childhood, be a sorry mess. Unwilling to admit the truth openly, he asserts that the old man is simply demented. Joshua has been used to interpreting life with respect to codes laid down by others, codes making for orderliness and regularity. Meanwhile, Labe, more malleable in personality, is unaware of such behavior standards and enters sympathetically into Alf's fantasy, even elaborating upon it.[19] Unlike his stiff-backed brother, Labe sees Alf not as odd but as companionable and imaginative; and he even promises to come back and visit him. The two brothers are finely differentiated characters.

No tragic human lesson is found in "The Pacing Goose," in which Eliza, who has a weakness for geese, sets out some goose eggs to hatch. Jess, who wants no such troublesome fowl underfoot, privily tells the hired man to pierce the shells secretly with a darning needle. Enoch bungles, somehow; one goose named Samantha is born, and rapidly grows under Eliza's feeding into a "full-rounded convexity"—"Emphasis on the vexity," complains Jess. The pet gives short shrift to his pansies, and it even intimidates him by extending its reptilian neck and blowing icy hisses at him. There is additional rustic humor after Samantha gets mixed up with geese on a neighboring farm and Eliza goes to court to recover her. " 'She's the only goose I ever heard of,' Eliza remembered mournfully, 'who'd drink tea.' "

As with some of the other stories, the reading pleasure resides especially in the *manner* of telling. There is a smiling literary allusiveness when Enoch, a reader of Emerson, thinks that some general information on women "might have a more than transcendental value." Besides enjoying a sensuous recital of back-country cooking, we also appreciate the sly wit involved when Jess, after he has complained that no one in the house has written any poetry despite the season's being spring, and then sniffs his wife's peach pies which are cooling, is informed by Eliza that he is like all men who want to have their poetry and eat it too.

There is no more thistledown delicacy of treatment in all the book than in "Lead Her Like a Pigeon," in which Mattie emerges into the nubile state and experiences her first maidenly uneasiness at having to leave home someday. The theme of approaching marriage, announced cumulatively, begins with the girl's spotting the pair of doves in the clearing near the empty house (this idea linked, too, with the bird image in the song heard later); her planning to care for the flowers growing untended in the yard (flowers symbolic of children); Jud Bent's references to her as Persephone, and to Gard Bent, the new boyfriend and future husband, as Pluto, who in mythology takes the goddess into the underworld as his wife; the love song beginning "Lead her like a pigeon," which she very much wants the boy with the horn to complete; and the still more conventional emblem of the wedding ring: "They [her maidenly hands washing dishes] could not play the tune she envied, the tinkling bell-like sound of her mother's wedding ring against the china . . . that said, I'm a lady grown and mistress of dishes and cupboards" (53-54).

Since Jessamyn West admits that Mattie is drawn after what she thought her mother might have been like as a girl living in that time,[20] it is natural to suspect that Gard Bent reflects Eldo West. As evidence of this source, we find that Gard has Indian blood and shares with Eldo West his farming background and his interest in schoolteaching.

In July, 1863, the Confederate raider John Hunt Morgan led a force of about 2,460 men from Kentucky to Vernon and, finding an armed militia lying in wait for him across the river, decided to bypass the town. This is the historical background of "The Battle of Finney's Ford" against which are played some moral decisions among the Birdwells as to whether a Quaker should forego his creed of nonviolence when safety demands a call to arms. Josh, moved by the state governor's appeal for militia, goes against his religious tradition and parental advice to join the local ragtag force. Although he never fires a shot against the enemy and although he ends up wounded from an inglorious fall off a cliff, he does have the satisfaction of overcoming fear and of proving himself a warrior. In putting aside the Quaker ideal, however, and rendering exclusively to Caesar, Josh foreshadows the increasing outer-directedness of the Friends that we find culminating in the mixed-faith marriage at the end of *Friendly Persuasion*, and in the spiritually impoverished community of *A Matter of Time*. Yet Josh is not the only physically brave member of his family: Labe is one who actually loves to fight; and his bravery, therefore, takes the form of self-control. We are led to believe that the author's heart is with Labe.

Jessamyn West, no exponent of heroics and physical violence, believes that courage can be shown just as easily without physical violence as with it. Unquestionably, a natural feminine aversion to the games of war as well as a predictable Quaker quietism, to say nothing of hewing to a historical account in which no battle even occurred at Vernon, conspired to debar her from the subject of physical conflict. Another explanation is that she had early taken up a personal interest in Stoicism as a philosophy to live by, such a belief making her lot as an invalid endurable. The philosophy carries over into the portrayal of her literary figures.[21] The present Birdwell story is, consequently, not likely to satisfy the reader who demands raw action in the place of, or following upon, moral decisions, especially as the author does build up to a battle scene and then defeats expectation.

In contrast, "The Buried Leaf" is a quiet interlude among the selections. At the outset, Mattie is vexed at her father's refusal to let her change her name to something she thinks is elegant. After sulking, she and Little Jess unearth in an abandoned cellar a box containing a leaf from the Bible that sets a new value upon her name. From an anecdote told her by her father, she learns how heroic her ancestors, including a cousin Mattie, had been in the wilderness.

"A Likely Exchange" and "First Day Finish" are companion pieces about horses; and they are so vividly wrought that some of the author's relatives believe—despite the almost totally fictional basis—that such happenings did occur. In the first piece, Jess, alone on a business trip in rural Kentucky, skillfully trades his own slow carriage horse for an unsightly quadruped whose only good point is refusing to be passed on the road. This neatly satisfies his wife's injunction on parting, that he get rid of their "racy-looking animal," and at the same time gratifies his own lurking desire for a beast that can outrace the Reverend Godley's Black Prince. It just so happens that the owner, a Mrs. Hudspeth, wants a slow pacer, one slow enough to be no obstacle in marrying off her four big, husky, pipe-smoking, and, in short, barely marriageable daughters. As she phrases it with good West psychology, "Men ain't got any heart for courting a girl they can't pass—let alone catch up with" (114).

In the second story, the now successful horse trader drives his ungainly animal to victory the Sunday after he returns home; astonishes Eliza, who had not planned on ripping off to church in a cloud of dust; and quite frustrates the sleek, smug Methodist preacher who had expected to tear past them as usual on his way to harangue his congregation. Although not intended to be that way, the race becomes an interdenominational contest, the outcome of which even the sober Quaker congregation accepts with unspoken but sure content.

There are various ways of creating the verisimilitude of a horse race, such as using long, sustained sentences that gallop along breathlessly, flinging the lather of rhetoric into the air. Twain shows how it is done with the pony express rider early in *Roughing It*. Miss West's sentences are not, however, distinguished by this method; her effects stem largely from a suspense carefully built up, beginning with the first of these two stories; subtlety of phrase, rather than power of large units of rhetoric; and, lastly, a confident knowledge of horseflesh.

Like the two selections just examined, " 'Yes, We'll Gather at the River' " contains a strain of frontier humor in the tradition of such early practitioners as George Washington Harris, Augustus B. Longstreet, and Johnson J. Hooper. As proof of this similarity, there is the interest in rural speech extending here to the Quaker's "thees" and "thous"; the suggestion of the coarse, adding Realism; the crude and decidedly comic figure; the practical joke leading to bodily discomfiture; and, finally, the roughhouse revenge giving rise to laughter.

The unclean hayseed Lafe Millspaugh, who had acquired some thirty years earlier a dread of bath water, is hired to build Jess a bathhouse on the porch—the first chamber of its kind west of the Ohio. Conservative Eliza opposes the project, for fear the neighbors will talk. First it was music, then horse racing, and now a tub for bathing (and for singing in, too?)—a luxury that is too lax for the teachings of the early church! Lafe takes his own opposition too far by deliberately leaving out a door for the completed "carnal room," whereupon Jess treats him to a surprise dunking in the tub. As usual with Miss West's technique, the author does not report the physical struggle directly but reveals it filtered, second-hand, through the senses of a nonparticipant, Eliza. Actually, the tiff turns out to be quite funny this way. Such an auctorial withdrawal from anything approaching violence reminds us of the practice of Willa Cather in *Death Comes for the Archbishop*.

Now past middle age, Jess in the following story is initially worried about an enormous wen on his neck. "The Meeting House" opens symbolically with him at the fireside extending his fingers as if to gather warmth in them. Although he had planned to take a sentimental trip to a distant meeting house where his parents had worshiped, he never gets there; instead, he has some encounters along the route that remind him of the threat of death that faces even the young. In the house of one of his customers, tiny, seven-year-old Jasper Rice lies dying in a bed far too big for him. "A poor peaked little grain of Rice for such a big conveyance," is Jess's metaphysical observation, this last being about as close to sentimentality as the story ever gets (149). An equally pathetic case is Mrs. Rivers, a dying young woman deserted by her husband who, unable to bear the presence of sickness, has to find some consolation in a mistress. True here to the practice throughout *Friendly Persuasion* as well as in other fictional works, Jessamyn West forebears to judge the morals or indiscretions of her people and presents everything objectively.

The upshot of Jess's trip is that, when he compares his anxiety over the wen to the suffering he found in other people, he thinks himself fortunate indeed; he signals his renewed delight in the simple and beautiful things of this world by sniffing the lilies-of-the-valley newly opened at home. As is again characteristic of a West story, this delight is disclosed by implication, not by open assertion. Very likely, an archetype exists somewhere for the plot here—the current interest in archetypal criticism may uncover one someday—yet the telling has an authentic freshness for all that.

Kept indoors by rain one day, Jess in "The Vase" shows an idle interest in a vase Eliza has left half-finished long years before. Here, the viewpoint shifts easily and unobtrusively to that of Eliza for whom the vase, made from a cracked lamp shade, holds sentimental associations. To her the object recalls the enthusiasm, the bouquet, of her early married days when before her gleamed, as it so often does in youth, an ideal future wherein chance sorrows are mercifully kept out of sight. The swan, accordingly, is emblematic of that dream: the swan painted upon a shade whose crack is hidden with decoration. We are told in flashback that shortly after the infant Sarah died, she had begun work upon the companion swan on the shade, but was understandably interrupted by Jess one wintry day when he came in to lament the snowflakes that were then covering up Sarah's grave. The second swan consequently remained "gray and shadowy . . . reminding her of so much, the dream before sunup . . . ," meaning the imperfectly fulfilled future as the counterpart of the earlier vision. The theme here includes the life cycle with its attendant joys and sorrows.

Admittedly, the ostensible event in "The Illumination" is a gathering of neighbors in Jess's house to celebrate the advent of his gas lighting; but the essential interest, as with so many of the narratives, lies in character revelation. There is a sharp moral contrast implicit in Jess, a man more than pleased to spend his money for such a sensuous satisfaction as gas light, and in the miser Whitcomb, who refuses to buy himself any luxuries at all. Part of the success in sketching Whitcomb lies in making him no stock figure, no ordinary miser. The author probes at least far enough into his makeup to enable the reader to respond with pity rather than contempt. Both men are sadly aware of the winging away of years, the waiting dust; still, they strive in their markedly different ways to preserve something of value from the Heraclitan flux. Jess, at least, now has in more ways than one a cheerful light to fend off the darkness. Another equally valid interpretation of the story is that Jess, a progressive, has to contend with the narrow-mindedness and back-wardness prevalent in some of his Midwestern neighbors.

Certain it is that the author has injected into her hero some of the sensibility and responsiveness of one of her favorite literary figures, Henry David Thoreau. Jess's sensitivity to natural beauty was mentioned earlier; but it is necessary to add that he, like many Friends in history, keeps a journal of spiritual observations (whimsically signing his sentences with famous men's names). Once he puts down a Thoreaulike "Eternity's the depth you go" and consents at last to sign his own name. When Eliza tells him that he ought to prepare his soul for the hereafter, he replies, while looking admiringly at the sky, "This is preparing," reminding us of Thoreau's confident "One world at a time." Like the inspector of snowstorms, he too is a high-minded epicurean who believes in getting a good taste of this world's pudding before passing on to the next world's ambrosia.

By the time we reach "Pictures from a Clapboard House," Mattie and Gard have long married. Just as the second story in the book is told from a youngster's point of view as he participates in an abortive shivaree, the child Elspeth in this antepenultimate idyll witnesses a successful shivaree during Christmas at the Maple Grove Nursery. Young Stephen Birdwell has returned from California to marry his non-Quaker fiancée, the wild, too-yielding, and none-too-faithful Lydia Cinnamond. No stickler about damaged goods or contraband, he marries her anyway against his parents' wishes.

Once again much depends on the device of perspective; and the child vision of Elspeth, to whom the serious palaver of the household is one with the glitter of snowfall, the Christmas tree shine, the untying of presents, and the shivaree, has all the cinematic flow of pictures that shimmer with a radiance known best to one in the morning of life. The juxtaposition of the wondering and trusting innocence of Elspeth with the catlike softness and inconstancy of experienced Lydia gives to these charming pictures just the faintest touch of Realism. The author uses the child essentially as a lens through which we may discern the patterns of adult behavior; and we may judge it if we choose but no more harshly than would the child.

Elspeth, representing the third generation of Birdwells in the book, is a link in the chain of eternity. Ever so sensitively Miss West sketches at the outset the image of the child seated in the parlor stringing popcorn harness for the Christmas tree: Elspeth thinks of her absent mother (second generation) as the clock ticks slowly "For-ev-er . . .for-ev-er"; under this spell, she understandably feels lonely with her mother gone and with the tick-tock of everlastingness insinuating itself in her ear; and, feeling a need for human affection as a hedge against a chilling eternity, she asks her grandmother if she loves her. "Better than I did my own," Eliza was used to replying to such a question, for "Then I was too young . . . to know childhood wasn't enduring" (187). Though too much the child to comprehend—and this immaturity is what makes the situation poignant—the granddaughter unreflectingly occupies her own place in the long procession of generations that move from the cradle to the casket. Even so, the story's tone is quite cheerful.

The account of Homer Perkins in "Homer and the Lilies" is perhaps the most touching narrative in *Friendly Persuasion*. An adopted twelve-year-old lad, he is as curious as the once-youthful Jess had been concerning all that is strange and beautiful in the world about him; but his misfortune is that the kindly couple he lives with are dead to speech and to wonder. The ordinary, to Homer, is transfigured. He questions eagerly about natural phenomena—whether a mouse can run backward—and listens with breathless delight to the whispery fall of first snowflakes upon the roof just over his attic bed. In this lovable boy, and lovable twice over because the reader can see in him the best part of his own real or imagined youth, Jess recovers the boyhood he had once known. We accomplish this seeing without the slightest intrusion of the sentimental.

One day in the woods Homer makes friends with the nurseryman, who is a match for him in Wordsworthian sensitivity. In an unconscious farewell gesture to this world—managed with the author's usual understatement—Homer one day pulls up and clutches to him an armful of Eliza's lilies simply because they ravish him with their scent and loveliness. Jess's reproof on that occasion is poignant when we look back on it, for not long afterward, during a winter storm, the little boy passes away. By means of allusive wording Jessamyn West succeeds in conveying the impression, ever so gently, that Jess himself has not many winters to go. In a symbolic sense, he has died vicariously through Homer. On the literal level, the sad imminence of his own demise is postponed yet awhile, enabling the group of stories to end on just the right bittersweet note. And the already wise Jess is wiser still.

It takes no great insight to learn that the plots in these stories are usually slight; for the focus is on some revealing incident or revelation in the life of one or more of the principal characters, a technique placing Jessamyn West in the mainstream of twentieth-century short-story writing. There are three serious themes in the book. The first concerns the adolescent confronted with the problems of adulthood. We can see this theme in "Shivaree" and in "The Battle of Finney's Ford," where the Quaker conscience is at odds with the demands of manhood and patriotism. The second and third themes are closely related; the second is the eternal procession of mankind enacted by the various Birdwells and their acquaintances who either pass through the normal life cycle or, who as with Jess and especially Elspeth, represent links in the long human chain. Several stories here are the more affecting for being bathed in the light of eternity. This theme brings us naturally to the last theme, that of illumination, as in "The Meeting House" and "Homer and the Lilies." In the former story, contact with the dying young acts reflexively to produce in Jess a heightened esthetic sense; in the latter story, the demise of Homer brings on in the nuseryman a spiritual change, one more fitting now that Jess is presumably at the ripe age for wisdom and for meeting his Maker. As suggested earlier, we cannot help thinking that the constant threat of death in the author's own experience conditioned her to create literature in which human beings are, as Victor Hugo felt about mankind in general, under a glorious reprieve from the sentence of death.

As for the sources of the book, Miss West accounts for them summarily in *To See the Dream*: "*The Friendly Persuasion*, insofar as it is anyone's experience, is the experience of my great-grandparents as remembered by my mother from tales told her by her parents.... The facts are very few . . ." (132-33). And the facts are that, in this "love poem to Indiana," as the author felicitously calls it, Jess is modeled upon her great-grandfather, Joshua Vickers Milhous, a nurseryman near Vernon.[22] Joshua had such a passion for music that on one of his visits to Indianapolis he bought a two-hundred-and-sixty-dollar Mason and Hamlin organ; and, of course, his Quaker minister-wife, Elizabeth, objected, as did the congregation. Even though the Quaker neighbors never became accustomed to the instrument, the Milhous children were delighted, as was their mother in time. Nevertheless, the whole affair of Quigley and the church elders in "Music on the Muscatatuck" is fiction.[23]

Like Jess, Joshua had a love for flowers and birds and was enthusiastic about stargazing. He was supposed to have enjoyed fast horses, but the races in the book are pure inventions. The same applies to the Kentucky trip. " 'Yes, We'll Gather at the River' " derives partly from an experience Joshua had in building a bathroom; he had a tiff with the carpenter, who had refused to install a door because the specifications did not call for it. And "The Illumination" draws upon Joshua's successful installation of manufactured gas in his home. Left out of the story is the unpleasant fact that fumes began to rise into the house from a storage tank underneath and necessitated removing the equipment—much to Eliza's relief.

The personality and appearance of Eliza are indebted to the Mary Frances McManaman mentioned earlier, a black-haired Irish woman who made vases from lamp chimneys. The names Eliza, Mattie, Jess, and Josh are all derived from Miss West's ancestors.

There was no shivaree at a bachelor's house. Grace West had told her daughter about an old man near the Maple Grove Nursery who used to talk to an imaginary spouse. As said before, Grace forms the basis for Mattie's characterization. "My mother," writes Jessamyn West in a letter to the author of this book, "riding a white horse carried cookies in a reversed footstool to an ailing woman in the woods." Grace remembered a neighboring orphan boy of sixteen or seventeen named Homer. In spite of apparent good health, Homer was found one morning dead in bed—there was no evidence of foul play. Grace saw him in the coffin in his front yard with white tube roses in his hand. "The whole story came from the wonder in her voice at this sight. . . ."

"The Buried Leaf" owes its being to the author's memory of her own girlhood when she saw in the cellar of a house a Bible left to molder. "Pictures from a Clapboard House" has a similarly faint origin in the author's experience, in this case from hearing over the telephone in the grandmother's house the clock ticking in her own house. And "The Battle of Finney's Ford" is all fiction except for Morgan's raid.

As we may observe, the facts are indeed skimpy. Far from being family history, or even an attempt at it, *Friendly Persuasion* is almost totally a product of the imagination; to insist otherwise is to grossly underestimate what it entails to convert a "germ," as James calls it, into an artistically wrought story. In the total context of her output, the book is as exquisitely wrought as anything Miss West has published.

Inasmuch as Jessamyn West left Indiana very early, apparently before she gained any unfortunate impressions of the region applicable to her time or before, she could well afford to look back with romantic nostalgia. We may well wonder what kind of Birdwell collection would have resulted had Miss West revisited North Vernon *before* the writing began. An earlier Quaker author, James Baldwin (1841-1925), spent his entire youth in central Indiana in the area around Westfield. His highly autobiographical narrative, entitled *In My Youth From the Posthumous Papers of Robert Dudley*, was later reissued with the significant subtitle: *An Intimate Personal Record of Life and Manners in the Middle Ages of the Middle West.*[24] This novel furnishes a quite different view of pioneer life during the period that corresponds with the young manhood of Jess Birdwell. It is the viewpoint of an "insider." Jess and his family, we will remember, seem to be somewhat isolated but not lonely, have a simple yet not drab environment, and soon come to know the beauty of music and the luxury of a bathtub and gas lighting. *In My Youth*, in contrast, shows a shy, sensitive boy starved for beauty and oppressed by the harsh realities of a pioneer Quaker settlement. Mercifully, he escapes into a world of fantasy where he has imaginary playmates to keep him company and somehow make life bearable. Still, the lad takes a cheerful view of Quaker life on the frontier, despite the numberless privations—yes, including that of music. Probably there is no more hauntingly R alistic contrast with Miss West's book to be found anywhere in the limited body of Hoosier-Quaker literature.

Widely translated abroad (Dutch, French, German, Spanish, and Italian editions appeared in 1945), *Friendly Persuasion* soon established Jessamyn West as the most accomplished Quaker author of the age; and the reputation of this book overshadowed most, if not all, of her later non-Quaker work. Perhaps the motion picture, as well as the catchy theme song from it, "Thee I Love," which was heard over the radio even a decade later, helped create this imbalance.[25]

III   The Friendly Persuasion: *Film*

Early in 1955, when Miss West was busy assembling *South of the*

Angels, the producer-director William Wyler of Allied Artists Productions engaged her to come to Hollywood and to prepare a shooting script of *Friendly Persuasion*. She agreed, although she knew the
book resisted film adaptation because of its lack of story continuity.

Miss West chose the Civil War material for the central episode,
and she invented many new scenes as well as transformed for her
purpose incidents from various stories in the collection. When the
resulting script grew too long, a Mr. Kleiner was assigned to prune
it; then, when he failed, she was brought back to the task as col-
laborator. Finally, the director's brother was also set to work on it.
In *To See the Dream* she reports how she held out for the conception of Jess as a conscience-bound pacifist and would not allow the
director to embroil him in a fight. Luckily, she was able to help stop
more than one philistine-inspired alteration of her script: for example, the director had planned to have Jess, the mighty pacifist,
destroy all by himself a manned battery of Confederate cannon and
to do so without lifting his fist or firing a single shot. Miss West's
problem was the greater because the leading role was to be played
by the popular Gary Cooper, a fortunate choice as it turned out,
whose public (he reminded her) demanded that he be a man of
action and *do* something.

In August, after nine months of collaboration, the script was
ready—subject, of course, to various important changes made "on
location." The next month the filming of the nursery scenes began
at California's Rowland Lee Ranch, and the battle scenes were made
on the banks of the Sacramento ten miles out of Chico. Finally,
after a reputed cost of $3,200,000, the motion picture was presented
in 1956.

There are enough noticeable resemblances between the book
and the film to remind the reader pleasantly of his adventures with
the text without constituting a repetition; yet there are more than
enough differences to satisfy him that the film has a new story to
tell. A broad, folksy, sometimes sexy humor replaces wit for the
most part; Little Jess and the Hudspeth daughters assume comic
roles; the budding love between Mattie and Gard comes to full
blossom; the character Labe (replaced by a friend called Caleb)
and at least ten other figures disappear altogether. The film keeps
the "thees" for the sake of authenticity and quaintness; and, in the
same spirit, it gives the Quakers some colorful costuming (true to
history!), the color vividly heightened, of course, through the use

of Vista Vision photography. And, true to Hollywood's concept of real colorfulness, the trees have been sprayed with a green dye.

Incidents retained from the book include the horse trading and racing, the quarrel over the organ (Eliza, in anger, stalks to the barn to spend the night, soon joined by her husband, who effects in the straw an amorous reconciliation), the call of the church elders, and Josh's riding to war. The camera eye, necessarily limited in what it can record, renders little account of the esthetic and philosophic side of the remarkable nurseryman of the book.

Events in the screenplay are arranged to make it more and more tempting, even urgent, for Jess to take up his rifle against Morgan's men, especially after Sam Jordan (new name for Reverend Godley) is killed and Josh's horse gallops home riderless. In a final scene he does compromise to the extent of going armed to the battlefield to search for his son while the fight still rages; and there he encounters a bushwhacker whom he is provoked to disarm and whose life he then spares.

The motion picture deservedly became a popular success and moved up to candidacy for a Motion Picture Academy Award, in spite of the stance of smug superiority taken by the reviewer in *Time* magazine that year.[26] But it lost the award to the lengthy and inferior *Around the World in Eighty Days*. The Quakers gave *The Friendly Persuasion* a mixed reception, although two of their journals, at least, did carry extremely favorable reviews.[27] Most likely the film enhanced the Quaker image here and abroad. With certainty this very first venture in screenwriting marked a triumph for Jessamyn West. And when the motion picture first appeared in her home town of Whittier, the local theater ran to full house several times during more than a week of showings.[28]

IV *Further Persuasion*

In the spring of 1969, almost a quarter of a century after the publication of *Friendly Persuasion*, Harcourt, Brace issued her second and what will probably be the final installment of Birdwell pieces, *Except for Me and Thee*. More than half these had never been printed before and had been written expressly for the book—an unprecedented method for Miss West. Gaps in the previous collection were filled in. Sarah and Gard had had roles that were barely sketched; now these figures are enlarged. Perhaps due to the scriptwriting influence, both Little Jess and the Civil War take on increased significance. In the first collection, the reader was left curious about Jess's bachelor days—about how he met Eliza, about the manner of courtship, and about why they moved from Mount Pleasant, Ohio, to the homestead at Vernon. The new collection more than satisfies these needs. And, for the first time, a West book handles that infamous contradiction in the land of freedom and egalitarianism, Negro slavery.

By midsummer this new assemblage had the ephemeral distinction of being on several best-seller lists; it competed for favor with such novels as Vladimir Nabokov's *Ada* and Philip Roth's incredibly filthy *Portnoy's Complaint*. Unquestionably, Miss West's family relationship to the newly elected president of the United States, Richard Nixon, had some favorable effect on sales, especially after her appearance on the National Broadcasting Company's televised "Today" show. Even more potent as advertising must have been the long-time popularity of *Friendly Persuasion* both as a book and as a film. Moreover, the new book fortunately came out at a time when the reading public was jaded with a superfluity of raw stories about sex, perversion, and brutality; consequently, it found a welcome, not only because it was a well-written book about a family that held interest, but because it reaffirmed a belief in a more normal, peaceful, even charming mode of existence.

The character types, the main locale, the back-country Quaker diction, the rustic drollery and high jinks, and even the situations are agreeably consistent with those of the 1945 collection. The book is warmhearted but unsentimental, kindly, folksy, comfortable; and, in those stories about slavery and war, we find compassion for the victims. At times there is a dark seriousness which in the first edition is only hinted at. Thus the reader finds here and there a reaction against the idealized material of *Friendly Persuasion*, a reaction consisting of increased Realism and a critical awareness that Quakers must somehow, short of violence, come to grips with, and if possible alleviate, the social evils of their age. There is less poetry now, and the style is not so light and graceful as in 1945. On the other hand, there is more wisdom and humaneness, together with what Matthew Arnold would have called the ability to see life whole.

Because we have already discussed numerous features of most of the *Friendly Persuasion* series, we cover the new pieces in a cursory fashion. "The Wooing," the first of the new set, shows Jess as a restless swain who rebels, though but briefly, against the Quaker tradition of marrying only within the sect; for "He intended to live, not to repeat a pattern" (8). His wildest fling consists of letting himself get intoxicated in the company of a husband-hungry girl, acceding to her proposal, and the next day getting betrothed to still another girl. Some light comedy develops when the two prospective brides, having learned of each other's troth, walk sorrowfully up to the Birdwell dinner table together and require Jess to make a choice. He turns them both down, for by this time he has fallen in love with the woman preacher, Eliza Cope. At the opening of the next story, he and Eliza have been married for five years and are chafing at having to live in father-in-law Birdwell's house. Jess now takes a long trip into the West to look for a suitable homesite, and he picks a fertile and beautiful spot in Indiana, which becomes the Maple Grove Nursery. "The New Home," third in the group of stories about Jess's early life and his settling near Vernon, is chiefly memorable for the figure of the lightning-rod salesman Herman Leutweiler, who has all the glib cunning and racy speech of Professor Quigley, and then some. Naturally, Jess must safeguard his new house from chain, sheet, and ball lightning.

"First Loss" is about the death of their firstborn, Sarah, victim of scarlet fever at age five. The coffin symbolism here is eerily effective. Following this sad episode there is the relatively inconsequential "Mother of Three" whose only excuse for being seems to be that it represents for the first and only time in the whole series the everyday trial of a young mother in rearing an obstreperous brood of children who sometimes get into mischief. The happenings are as domestic as buckwheat pancakes; still, we might consider them trivial. Yet how much of the daily living on the nineteenth-century American frontier—minus the occasional "inner light," Indian raids, wars, and the founding of homesteads and communities—could not be considered trivial? The marvel is that Miss West can make intriguing these sober, God-fearing, orderly, practical and artistically starved Quakers whose actual counterparts in history (the Milhouses) were reportedly, with rare exceptions, anything but imaginative and spirited.

"Neighbors," by far the longest episode in the book, is one of the best. The setting is 1856. Despite the tone of calculated understatement and domesticity conveyed by the title, the action is full of physical excitement and suspense as Eliza and her neighbors save a Negro slave couple from recapture. The turning point in the drama comes when Eliza is forced to admit, in the face of her conservatism and respect for legal authority, that there is a higher moral law to which the cruel Fugitive Slave Law must submit. The author makes her, rather than Jess, the focus of narration, perhaps for the reason that Eliza had not earlier committed herself to any serious social problems or had any brush with danger. *Except for Me and Three* might be subtitled *Eliza's Coming Out*. A later adventure in which she again involves herself in the alleviation of human misery is "After the Battle," the battle being Morgan's raid, in which she binds the wound of a young Rebel trooper.

Jess in "Fast Horseflesh" gets his warmup for the race against Godley's Black Prince, whose defeat was covered in *Friendly Persuasion*. A newspaper editor named Arkell wins over him, evidently because Eliza, who wanted to teach her husband a lesson, prayed for the opponent's horse. Or it might be that Red Rover is simply a poor racer; he is traded later in the Hudspeth episode for Lady. Meanwhile, Jess hatches a scheme for at least keeping Eliza from praying *against* his animal.

The weakness of using Jess exclusively as the focus of narration keeps "Growing Up" from being as funny or at least as satisfying as it might otherwise be. Some comic possibilities were lost in not permitting the reader to follow young Labe to his birthday party at Louella's where, for all we know, the amorous seamstress might have given Labe some awkward moments. It stands to reason, too, that the emotional impact of growing up, of a lad's being pursued by an older woman, ought to be keener in the participant than in the parents. Of course it is more difficult to depict, too, but Miss West would have solved this problem admirably had she not decided to restrict the focus of narration throughout the book to either Jess or his wife. "Shivaree before Breakfast," in the other collection, is a good example of how the direct initiatory experience in the young can be presented movingly without any intervening consciousness of the Birdwell parents to provide interpretation; there, Josh and Labe are constantly before the reader, for their feelings, rather than the parents' possible response to the adventure with Old Alf, constitute the main interest.

It might as well be observed at this juncture that one of the biggest differences between the volumes of 1945 and 1969 is just this striving after a consistent focus of narration by showing every adventure as it impinges upon either Jess or Eliza or both. (As hinted earlier, this focus is sometimes gained at a loss in dramatic power.) *Friendly Persuasion* deviated from this "ideal" at least four times; *Except for Me and Thee*, devised after many years of teaching creative writing in the universities, of building novels, and of contriving coherent motion-picture scripts, demonstrates a tight method of unifying an episodic story line. The fact that so many of the new stories were written in the first place for a collection promoted unity. Whereas, the separate parts of *Friendly Persuasion*, designed for scattered magazines over the years, ranged at large by focusing on three generations of Birdwells.

"A Family Argument" reveals Jess as a wise patriarch who holds his family together in time of dissension by firm will and fair-minded behavior. Like the nation still smarting from the trials of the Civil War just ended, the Birdwells have their internal quarrels too. And the years have brought changes: Mattie has married, yes, a Methodist; her Gard is now a farmer; Little Jess has grown into a pert youngster who likes to interrupt discussions; and Josh attends school in Philadelphia. Compared with Jess, all the young people present to celebrate his birthday seem foolish; they are, like puppies, growling over a rag and tearing it apart. Still, he refuses to wax bitter and complain: "The world suits me to a T, Mattie. That's my trouble. Why, sometimes I think the Lord made it especially for me. I like its colors. I don't see how the flavor of spring water could be improved on. I'd hate to have to try to invent a better fruit than a Grimes Golden. Yellow lamplight on white snow. Thee ever seen anything prettier?" (283).

In the final story there is a moral of a kind to confirm Jess in his contentment. Two related plots operate, one inside the other, to treat the theme of family love. "Home for Christmas" finds Jess resisting Mattie's request to put up a Christmas tree (Methodist bauble)—Quaker tradition did not provide for this modernism. With the tree would come Christmas stockings and presents, other innovations having nothing to do with true Christmas spirit! "The bigger the celebration in the world, Jess feared, the less chance the heart had for its celebrations" (294). But the tree, he knew, would make Mattie and her little Elspeth happy. At this juncture, the alcoholic Jasper Clark arrives to ask for a loan with which to buy his family Christmas presents. He gets it: Jess makes his first new step toward modernism. Not long afterward, Clarence Clark,

Jasper's son, clatters up to ask Jess to help deal with Jasper who, drunk now, has been shooting wildly from his upstairs window.

The true situation in the Clark family gradually unfolds for Jess after he reaches the scene. He learns that Jasper did not spend the borrowed money on liquor (someone gave him the jug), that he had remembered to buy presents for the whole family, and that his "stately dark-haired" wife Clara actually adores him. There is no sordid tragedy after all! Jasper's present spree was occasioned by learning that his Jenny is pregnant out of wedlock; he shoots to drive off her seducer should he come. Despite these misfortunes, the Clarks love and care for one another. But no sentimentality intrudes to mar the perfect dignity and restraint of those passages in which Jess and Clara converse about familial matters.

Back home, warmed by this example of domestic love, Jess permits the Christmas tree to be put up, although he does so against his better judgment. "People are getting more worldly every day," he laments with the expected conservatism of a grandfather. "Except for me and thee, Jess" (309), Eliza puts in, evidently speaking for the author herself, and incidentally providing the title for the book.

The only Birdwell story published earlier which was not included in the volume is "Little Jess and the Outrider," *Ladies' Home Journal*, LXXII (October, 1955). Not only is it inferior to "After the Battle" in bringing home to the Birdwell clan the reality of war but its inclusion would be repetitive, inasmuch as the theme of aiding a wounded trooper appears in both episodes. Besides, the focus in the omitted story is on Little Jess; *Except for Me and Thee*, as stated earlier, makes a point of limiting the focus to Jess and Eliza.

As a best seller, *Except for Me and Thee* obviously found some partisan reviewers. S. L. Steen in *Library Journal* wrote that the "characters are well portrayed, the prose poetic and charming with its Quaker idioms and touches of humor." In *Saturday Review*, Zena Sutherland notes the "vibrant authenticity of the characters . . . [and the] practiced ease and resilience of style." Perhaps it was Carlos Baker in the *New York Times Book Review* who gave the most thoughtful and sympathetic coverage of the book: he opined that readers will find out more about the Birdwells but have "a certain mild regret that [this] is not the equal of its predecessor. . . . What if this sequel is a little paler than 'The Friendly Persuasion'? . . . It will be a welcome accession to those (like myself) who are always eager to begin a new book by Jessamyn West." We might answer Mr. Baker by saying that *some* of the stories in the new book are finer than *some* in the old; and vice versa. The new book holds fewer surprises, true. For, after all, it was intended, as the subtitle suggests, as *A Companion to Friendly Persuasion.*

The two collections ought to be combined into one. An examination of all the stories shows clearly that a suitable order can be followed in such a gathering if he allows "Music on the Muscatatuck" to come first, as a beautifully seductive invitation to the series, and postpones "The Wooing," "Heading West," and "The New Home" until near the end where they could serve as a trio of connected flashbacks (which is what they now actually are). The newcomer to the now separate books might perchance find the following sequence helpful in his reading:

1. Music on the Muscatatuck
2. First Loss
3. Mother of Three
4. Neighbors
5. Shivaree before Breakfast
6. The Pacing Goose
7. Lead Her Like a Pigeon
8. Growing Up
9. The Battle of Finney's Ford
10. After the Battle
11. The Buried Leaf
12. Fast Horseflesh
13. A Likely Exchange
14. First Day Finish
15. "Yes, We'll Gather at the River"
16. The Meeting House
17. The Vase
18. The Illumination
19. A Family Argument
20. Home for Christmas
21. The Wooing
22. Heading West
23. The New Home
24. Pictures from a Clapboard House
25. Homer and the Lilies

V *The Buried Word*

An early unpublished story called "Footprints beneath the Snow" represents a first attempt to get at the materials of *The Witch Diggers* (1951).[29] In this twenty-two-page manuscript, nubile Lovetta Lewis, who is spending the Christmas holidays with her grandparents at the Jennings County Poor Farm, which the oldsters manage, so doubts that her lover Gardiner Bent will come to get her that she despairs. He is delayed because of a false report that she is spending Christmas with his rival. But, when in the dead of night, he at last arrives in his sleigh, she leaps out to him through the snow, and they ride off to a joyous reconciliation. The juxtaposition of youth with age, warm and passionate love with midwinter iciness, the lover arriving unexpectedly on one of the few nights of the year commonly devoted to celebration and hope (Christmas Eve), the maiden's sight of her future husband, the elopement from the bedroom, the old grandmother left behind to greet the chill of a winter morning—all these qualities are singularly evocative of Keats's tale of medieval elopement in "The Eve of Saint Agnes." Regardless, *The Witch Diggers* will show far fewer resemblances to the poem and must be considered completely original.

We may observe in this abortive story the Poor Farm of great-grandfather James McManaman's day, but it is suitably fictionalized even in this period when Miss West tended to be too transparently familial. There is a Jud Macmanaman as a carousing and bookish precursor to the serious and thoughtful Link Conboy of the novel; to their dissatisfied wives, both men represent an image of failure for having chosen the wrong line of work. The love situation using the ineligible suitor perhaps echoes Grace Milhous and Eldo West, who did some of their courting at the Farm.

"Footsteps beneath the Snow" already reveals the skillfull handling of folk speech that embellishes later works. The story is also interesting because it contains some of the materials that eventually were used in "Lead Her Like a Pigeon" and in "Pictures from a Clapboard House," a fact that shows that originally the substance of *Friendly Persuasion* and *The Witch Diggers* was hardly separable in the artist's mind. Creating Jess Birdwell and placing him at another ancestral location nearby no doubt cleared the way and left the Poor Farm with its figure of the waiting girl as a nucleus for a new, much longer story someday. The waiting girl became Cate Conboy.

A glimpse at the actual setting of *The Witch Diggers* may prove a diverting introduction to the plot summary that follows.[30] Not more than five miles of rolling country south of Vernon on Highway 7 in the direction of Madison, the visitor today sees on his left the prominent landmark of the Freedom Church, while on his right, a few hundred feet farther, lies the entrance to a gravel road. If he turns onto the road and winds with it a few minutes through

meager farmland and around a bend, he presently sees a two-story
red-brick edifice, shaped like an L, that sprawls at the far end of the
road. These acres, known as the County Farm, contain the only
red-brick building for miles around; it is a dilapidated, mysterious,
and lonely structure. In front, down a weedy declivity, Graham
Creek ripples its peaceful course through underbrush and among
scraggly trees.

Walking to the back of the building, the visitor finds the old place
in sad disrepair, unless the current owner has succeeded in making
his promised renovations. Still farther back across the red-clay
fields lies a small plot of land that the plowman always cuts around.
Here among the weeds and briars, as if to be neglected until Judgment Day, some dead have markers; others, lying under sunken
ground covered with thorn and weed, have not a slab to identify
them as the pauper inmates of the County Farm. These dead are
not blood brother to the self-sustaining, admirable peasants of
Thomas Gray's famous churchyard; still, if they could tell their
stories, the listener would doubtless hear the simple annals of the
needy and forlorn, the crippled and blind, the feeble-minded and
mad. Yet none of them, nor all of them taken together, would be
the story conceived by a certain transplanted Quaker fictionist who
had borrowed a few hints from her mother's yarns and had used
them for the building of a novel.

In the narrative of *The Witch Diggers*, which opens in Indianapolis during the Christmas season of 1899, twenty-two-year-old
Christian (Christie) Fraser boards a train headed south to visit Cate
Conboy, his new girl, at the mysterious Poor Farm. As a stranger
with at least average curiosity, he affords the reader fresh insight
into the place.

While en route there Christie recalls, in a flashback sequence,
his first meeting with Cate at a party in the home of his cousin
Sylvy Cope (the surname reappears in two other books) at Stony
Creek. Foreshadowings of death begin early in connection with
Christie: in his reflections, in his morbid talk with the cousin, and
some months later in a coffin episode; and the coffin appears again
several times.

The special weakness in Christie, as the bluff Uncle Wesley Cope
once told him, is that he cannot resist saying yes. The salesman fully
illustrates this weakness soon enough when he slips into bed with
the Uncle's own daughter, who is already in love with him and eager

67

to be married. The purpose of the bedroom scene is to show that Christie, unlike Ferris Thompson, his later rival for the hand of Cate, is a normal and passionate lover. By this time, Christie has already met Cate. He will soon get from her an invitation to visit that will end his dalliance with his cousin Sylvy and draw him into a web of relationships culminating in several broken hearts and in his own destruction.

Cate, four years Christie's junior, is second to her mother in being the best realized character in the novel. She is an egocentric, proud, boyish-looking (Conboy) girl with a superb figure, short curly hair, and dark flashing eyes. We may easily imagine that there is something of the young Jessamyn West in this attractive person. On the debit side of the ledger, Cate suffers from an indoctrination of her mother's sex fears. Successive events show that she represses her responsiveness in love, for to her sexuality is linked with pain and suffering.

Arriving at the Junction, Christie takes a macabre wagon ride out to the County Farm with the undertaker Korby, a vulgar social climber who is known for ostentatiously planting a kiss on the forehead of each and every corpse before closing the coffin. A chilling confrontation occurs when Christie is left holding a child's casket at the door of the main building, Korby having raced off suddenly, and when Dandie Conboy opens the door angrily to snatch the casket out of his hands.

We learn that Dandie, who insists on finding his own happiness without the aid of his altruistic father, has fallen in love with and, against his family's wish, will soon marry the softly feminine Nory Tate, a girl who had been raped and made pregnant by her uncle. Part of the story's suspense is whether or not Dandie will succeed in wringing from her the ravager's identity and what revenge he will then exact. (In Chapter 10 he castrates the old man.)

Another rebel is Cate's precocious little sister, Em, who pertly announces to Christie at their first meeting that she was probably adopted since she is so unlike the other Conboys. Em feels out of place at the house, for "she missed . . . those daily draughts of envy, admiration, and hate with which she was customarily refreshed at school" (202). Her innocent exhibitionism—drawing pubic hairs on herself with burnt match heads in order to seem grown up, and displaying herself naked to a peeping tom in an honest endeavor to cure him of his malady—is of course sensational yet still consistent with what we might expect of a well-meaning little flaunter living in such surroundings and developing, unlike her sister Cate, an uninhibited interest in sex. As with some of the other figures in the story, Em is engaged in a stumbling search for happiness; and her search is made all the more difficult because of her bizarre methods and the shocked disapproval of the family. Soon enough learning that she gets people into trouble by telling secrets, she learns to keep the important ones to herself, including the news that insane Mary Abel plans to destroy the pigs belonging to the Poor Farm.

Christie meets the parents as well. Lib, modeled somewhat after the author's mother,[31] is a handsome woman who enjoys being the Poor Farm's matron because of the social distinction. In the course of the narrative, she develops from a benevolent shrew, quick to belittle her husband, to a wifely companion who shows him genuine respect; and, from the unaffectionate mother of Cate, she becomes a creature of sorrow who pities her daughter and even kisses her for the first time. For Lib needs to feel superior to and have pity for others before she can ever show them affection. There is simply not space enough here to do justice to this provocative woman, to her pride and aloofness, her wrongheadedness yet capability for repentance, her vulgarity and slovenliness in keeping house, her capacity for insult, and her dexterity in putting presumptuous people in their place.

The problem with her husband, Link, is that he cannot get close to the souls of the inmates though he tries and tries. He has waited all his life to meet someone to whom he can open his heart. But his children are largely uncommunicative with him, Lib is too proud and distant (when not merely condescending), and most of the poor-house inmates are lame conversationalists. The only inmate with whom Link can communicate is John Manlief, an intelligent mute who miraculously regains his powers of speech from having bestowed love on a nursling pig that he has kept secreted in his room.

Among the grotesques cared for at the County Farm, Christie finds the cultists James and Mary Abel, brother and sister, who are obsessed with the simplistic idea that the Devil has long ago buried Truth somewhere in the earth and that what is now necessary is to dig it up so that mankind can again be happy. For this digging they try to recruit the young salesman who, unfortunately for them, has settled for the lesser happiness of making love to

Cate whenever he can get her alone; nevertheless, they do manage to enlist the adventuresome Em for their mad diggings. The activities of the witch diggers provide a symbolic parallel to the misguided and sometimes frantic efforts of the so-called normal persons, such as Cate, to reach happiness. After we read about Cate's foolish marriage, the Abels no longer seem quite so demented.

The main plot pertains to the courting and betrothal of Christie and Cate; her sudden renunciation of Christie, who is for her "that old darkness" which she feels she has to master and deny until she can enter safely, like a desexed nun, into the platonic bosom of the Thompson family where passion is not likely to appear; and her decision to marry the sensible, unexciting, and hypocritically delicate-minded Ferris Thompson. Ferris, she thinks, represents the antithesis of the loose and terrible sexual behavior that she is alarmed to find around her and even in her own ardent lovemaking (she once let Christie play with her breasts). Being almost sexless, Ferris would, consequently, be "good." In due course, she marries him, despite intelligent advice to the contrary from everyone; and she goes to live in the prissily inane household of domineering Mother Thompson, "a small, bow-legged woman who looked . . . a good deal like an anxious hen searching for a spot to drop an overdue egg" (136), and whose notion of housecleaning includes blowing dust from corners by means of a midget bellows.

Shocked at hearing of Cate's nuptials, the salesman gets drunk, is taken in by Sylvie, and the two are soon engaged to be married. Now that Cate has made a mess of her life, she at last realizes that she hates her husband and wants Christie. So she lures Christie to her with a letter. The plan almost works, except that he chances to visit Link at the Poor Farm first, where he loses his life trying to rescue livestock from the barn set afire by Mary Abel. His death leaves a guilt-stricken Cate who somehow has to apportion the blame and perhaps learn from wise John Manlief the right way to love.

The story is clearly a tragedy about an admirable girl who refuses to trust the honest dictates of her heart because of a mistaken notion about virtue—her "tragic flaw" is an error of judgment—and who consequently brings calamity upon herself and her true love. Like Emily Brontë's equally strange *Wuthering Heights*, the novel is about a passionate girl who learns too late that she has married the wrong man. Here in *The Witch Diggers* is the most carefully worked-out tragedy Jessamyn West has yet given us. From the death symbols at the beginning, all the way through to the conflagration, we feel a dark inevitability at work. The high point of mischief is the mistaken marriage, the death of love, aptly symbolized by the cooking of the goose named Eros. It is only a step further to the death of the lover himself. The witch diggers, who are on one level simply bizarre symbols of the mad quest for happiness in which Cate and Christie are to suffer, become in this intricately plotted novel instrumental as agents in the catastrophe at the end.

The sources of *The Witch Diggers* are interesting mainly insofar as they demonstrate how little of actuality Miss West chose to work with.[32] She made no interviews in or near North Vernon, she said; and she studied the administrations of none of the Poor Farm superintendents following MacManaman (she had never even heard of his immediate successors, O. M. Amick and Albert Ochs, until the author of this study told her about them). She admits having examined, during a visit at the Poor Farm, some nineteenth-century account books and having copied from them a few things such as "prices, items bought . . .whiskey, horse collars, rag carpets, etc.," along with some names of people associated with the asylum. On page fifty of the notebook used at the time, there is a list of nine inmates' names; comparison with the list on page 169 of the novel shows that she used three of them in altered form; three, unaltered. And of these characters only one, Lily Bias, is engaged in any kind of significant role. And where did the Conboy name come from? Although listed on the same page of the notebook as the other names—"Conboy for threshing 406 bu wheat 18.27"—the surname in the book derives from the childhood of the author when she heard her mother speak of going shopping at the "Conboy's" a country store in the Butlerville area.

Equally tenuous are other "facts" from the external world: (1) Grace West told her there were "witch diggers" in Jennings County somewhere, but she did not know why they dug or whether the diggers themselves knew. (2) A tobacco-chewing and promiscuous hired woman named Mag Ross worked for James MacManaman; unlike the jovially earthy Mag Creagan in the story, the original was old and unattractive. (3) Grace West also told her about the castration of a man in the county who was accused of incestuous relations with his daughter; nevertheless, this incident has no known connection with the Poor Farm. (4) Of the poor-house inmates, Miss West did learn from her mother about "Old Bob," or "Big Bob" as he was known during Ochs's administration, a Negro giant of dangerous temper and childish mentality, at whose death a coffin had to be specially made to be long enough for him. He figures several times in the novel. (5) Great-Grandmother MacManaman played Santa Claus to the paupers at Christmastime. (6) A North Vernon drunk, mentioned earlier, was the model for the ex-jockey Neddy Oates.[33] All else in the story was imagined—but this means practically everything.

And what an imagination! It runs into a riot of low comedy at times, as at the funeral service in the cemetery when the venereal Hoxie Fifield, tricked by an inmate into daubing his loins with turpentine as a medicine, races toward the group while doing awesome aerial stunts. Someone may object to this mixture of humor and solemnity. Yet humor is where an author finds it; even Shakespeare found it in a graveyard, and theater audiences have been praising the scene in *Hamlet* ever since. In general, Miss West's humor succeeds well when she handles low types (she never treats of upper-class life anyway), almost as if remembering the advice of Henry Fielding in *Tom Jones*, who says that "the highest life is much the dullest" and that "the various callings in lower spheres produce the great variety of humorous characters. . . ."

Even though the story never flags in human interest, never descends into mere sentimentality, and has merits beyond what this brief study has uncovered, it does not move the reader to the pitch of emotional involvement that the greatest literature does, as for instance Charles Dickens' *Little Dorrit* and Honoré de Balzac's *La Cousine Bette*. But most of the superior novels we read in a lifetime also do not reach that level. *The Witch Diggers* is a first novel, and it is a superbly structured one at that; and the first novels of several authors far more famous than Jessamyn West do not even come close to her achievement here.

The *donnée*, the search for happiness, is about as universal as any found among the acknowledged classics. Granting that Miss West stops short of offering neat answers, the reader is never left in doubt that what she is describing is a moral universe in which there is some kind of intelligent answer to human problems, but the answer may be as difficult to find as if the Devil himself had buried it in the bowels of the earth. With Miss West, love is the divining rod for finding such answers.

She wrote *The Witch Diggers*, she claims, "in an effort to become an 'honest woman' "; for she believed that *Friendly Persuasion* was not sufficiently Realistic—not typical of the impoverished and backward region of southern Indiana. Hence the novel would balance the account.[34] Hardly anyone would deny that she succeeded and then some.

That great dame of American letters, Eudora Welty, in one of the warmest of the predominantly favorable reviews of *The Witch Diggers*, remarked that the fault of each character lies in his inarticulateness—"from whence stems his fate and his disaster." This observation makes a good deal of sense if it is limited to the Conboy family. She also mentioned that Miss West created characters that are "alive and vividly struggling, explained fully"; nonetheless, the touch of mystery remains that surrounds real-life persons.[35] W. E. Wilson in *Saturday Review* (February 3, 1951) thought that the author fell a little short of the high mark set by her previous book, and this statement is about as severe as any the critics made. As could be expected, the Quaker press, in fact Quakers in general, tended to ignore the novel; maybe they felt that, if they looked the other way long enough, Miss West might reconsider this new direction that her craft was taking and come out with another innocuous, clean, untroubled idyll about the Quaker past.

The Witch Diggers did not sell well, and the reason is not easy to find. Surely the reason is not simply that it "wasn't dirty enough," as Miss West recently explained with facetious bitterness.[36] It could be that she had already created too indelibly the image of herself as the graceful, poetic Quakeress who writes with a Constablelike lovingness only of the beautiful past, of childhood, of horse races, and of other pleasant things.

VI An Experiment in Operetta

Hardly had *Friendly Persuasion* begun to grace the bookstores in 1945 when Raoul Péne duBois read a few pages of it and decided that this Californian would be the very person to write the words and lyrics to a musical he had in mind about Jean Jacques (John James) Audubon. She accepted his commission to do the work, for the artist-naturalist in her felt a kinship with the Haitian ornithologist whose portraits of American birds are among the nonpareils of rustic art. Her interests in this figure, and in Thoreau would meet in the study of nature, the love of freedom and life in the rough. DuBois arranged for the music to be written by Pulitzer Prize winner Gail Kubik.

By July of the following year her work was mostly done.[37] DuBois, as an independent New York City theatrical producer, doubtless had in mind the spatial resources of the large Broadway stage: "He told me not to hold back," Miss West was explaining years later on the eve of the world premiere, "because he could handle anything scenically."[38] His expansive instruction probably harmed the work by ignoring that need, evident now, to compress certain huge scenes and instill unity; yet, with orders to restrain herself, she might very well have refused the commission. The canvases turned out to be big—wagon train, river flatboat, forests—and the story embodied several ingredients of the Hollywood film-formula. The operetta interested a film company enough for it to invest one hundred thousand dollars in attempting its production, but the company finally abandoned the project because of formidable production problems.[39]

The piece as brought out in 1948 by her usual publisher, Harcourt, Brace and Company, carried the title *A Mirror for the Sky.*[40] It was illustrated by nine graceful costume sketches of the principal characters executed by duBois himself. Although the sub-title carries the word "opera," the work was delivered at its first performance under the label of "musical drama." However, of all the formal classifications of musical drama, the published and stage versions of *Mirror for the Sky* most resemble "operetta"—and this study, accordingly, refers to it that way—in being an amusing if somewhat sentimental play, with spoken dialogue, loose plot, arias, choruses, and dances; all in all, it stresses spectacle and music and it contains a happy ending.

Mirror for the Sky is a romantic story in fifteen scenes that depict the love life and artistic struggle of Audubon against a background of the American wilderness from 1808 to 1841. To facilitate an intrigue plot, the legend of Audubon's aristocratic birth is used. There is his courtship of Lucy Blakewell (historically, Bakewell), daughter of well-to-do parents, of which the father seems to like Audubon but cannot forgive him his poverty, whereas the mother accords him her unqualified disdain; the almost incredible faith and patience of Lucy following their marriage as she endures frontier hardships and defends her husband against charges of idleness and nonsupport; Audubon's refusal to compromise and become a well-paid portrait painter in Philadelphia; and, last, his belated recognition and fame.

Among the temptations and distractions strewn liberally in his path is the political intriguer Raynard, who promises the painter the restoration of his royal dignities in return for his supporting a popular revolution in France. This Raynard has no luck with the gifted immigrant who, having foresworn his noble pedigree is a staunch advocate of personal freedom—none, be it said, for the birds he has shot out of the trees, who must content themselves with immortality in his colored drawings. In one gay ballroom scene Audubon enunciates his sentiments clearly to some French aristocrats in the song (II, iv) commencing with "Freedom is a hard-bought thing." One temptation to which he does surrender is to accompany none other than Daniel Boone on an expedition to the West.

It should be no surprise that reviewers disagreed about the merits of this performance; for judging operetta as operetta, and not as regular stage drama, and without being able to listen to or read the music or see the stage spectacle, poses special difficulties. A sensitive critic could surely enjoy reading some of the songs even though he did not know the tunes. A good example is the witty song sung by Wayland Platter (I, v).

The stage production came about practically by accident. Horace W. Robinson, the director of the University Theater at the University of Oregon, chanced upon a copy of the play in a second-hand bookstore and wrote to Gail Kubik to learn about the music. About six years later, Robinson and his committee, after again reading the libretto, decided to present a mammoth public performance on May 23 and 24, 1958, in the large field house called McArthur Court on the university campus. This would not only be the biggest stage show in the history of Eugene, Oregon, but the first time the university had tried a work never before presented upon the stage. McArthur Court could seat an audience of five thousand and have room for the two-hundred-and-fifty-voice University Chorus, the sixty-two-member University-Eugene Symphony Orchestra, and a cast of thirty-two actors and sixty-nine extras, not to mention dozens of production and business-staff people along with a profusion of stage properties.

Chosen to play Audubon was a graduate student named Phil Green, a baritone who had played in almost three dozen musical comedies, and operettas and who had also sung with the Robert Shaw Chorale and the American Opera Society. A beautiful undergraduate with experience in summer theater work, Josephine Verri, would play Luci.

In spite of insufficient time for rehearsals the operetta opened on the evening of May 23 as planned. The extensive publicity and promotion of this work in the local newspaper, on television and radio, and by flyers and letters brought in about three thousand customers for the opening performance; and seated in the audience were Jessamyn West and Gail Kubik. Perhaps it was just as well that no professional dramatic critic was present. After the intermission, vacant seats were "very obvious," according to one customer who was shocked at how the Eugene *Register-Guard* in its review the next day played down the shortcomings of the entertainment.[41] One person there, supposedly exceedingly knowledgeable about dramas, had this to say: "It was a bomb. It was ill-fated because of the place (McArthur Court . . .where it was staged). The extraordinary nature of the production tended to de-emphasize the story and emphasize the spectacular."[42]

To Mr. Robinson, one of the principal criticisms offered by patrons was the difficulty in following the story, in keeping the characters straight, and in understanding their relationships. He adds that the music was "magnificent"; but, being quite modern and sophisticated, it was not especially suited to the rustic quality of the libretto, which is surely a period piece. Moreover, in the production the music and libretto tried to "out do each other in terms of time and in terms of consequence." Having watched the premiere, Miss West allegedly confessed to Mr. Robinson that she, too, was dissatisfied with her piece and knew some ways in which to improve it.[43] Insofar as is known to me, the operetta has never been repeated elsewhere, although the Roger Wagner Chorale has employed some of the songs in its programs.

One criticism of Robinson's is particularly valid: the lack of continuity. Any reader of the book can see that Audubon and Lucy are quickly swallowed up by the spectacle of the great American wilderness, its colorful humor, its singing, its restless movement of flatboat and wagon train. Some of the scenes are not strictly essential; and the scenes, taken as a whole, do not contribute toward any single dramatic action but, instead, relate to a whole lifetime of artistic perseverance and wifely fidelity. Probably a single great episode from Audubon's life would have provided the limitation of scope and the unity which are needed. On the other hand, if conservatively staged, the work as it exists ought to prove entertaining.

VII   *Circe at Whitewater*

Jessamyn West's latest novel, *Leafy Rivers* (1967),[44] is alluded to in the writing notebook as an entry written down some fifteen or twenty years before. The entry reads simply: "A story in the past—the woman who drove the pigs." This story must have given her more than the usual amount of labor; and, even before she had completed the manuscript, she was placing less value on it than on, say, *A Matter of Time*,[45] which is covered later in connection with the California items.

The novel deals only in part with the Indiana scene, namely the Connersville area together with the stretch of oak and beech forests edging south along the Whitewater River to Cincinnati. The state of Ohio figures in the opening and closing scenes.

And, in the opening scene, buxom young Leafy is about to give birth to her first child at her mother's home in Blue Grass, Ohio, where she is visiting for a few weeks before returning with her incompetent husband to their Indiana homestead. Only Leafy knows that the father of the child is not her husband.

The narrative, told from the omniscient point of view, finally reverts to the recent past after Leafy's family with their biographies and problems are introduced. While waiting and waiting for Leafy's child to arrive—it will be a difficult birth—we slip back into 1816 and follow Leafy and her husband, Reno Rivers, into the Hoosier state where they (mostly Leafy) run a pig farm for a year while endeavoring to make the place pay for itself. The reader learns that their Whitewater landlord, the lonely widower-sheriff Simon Yanders, falls in love with Leafy and dares to kiss her one day; that, when a debt becomes overdue and the sheriff tries to enforce payment by seizing their livestock, she tricks him into the barn, locks him up, steals his horse, and sets out alone to drive the pigs to Cincinnati where she will sell them to pay off their debt.

Along the trail her herd roots out a nest of snakes, the old Edenic symbol of sin. Like the stolen kiss, the snakes represent an appropriate forshadowing of fallen virtue. A storm soon makes the girl take shelter in a fancy covered wagon, actually a boudoir on wheels, owned by handsome pig-drover Cashie Wade. As mistress of Cashie on the trip and as controller of pigs, Leafy now assumes the aspect of Circe. Hanging just beneath the wagon is a wire-enclosed pen for carrying sick pigs: it is no accident in this thickly symbolic story that the bed of adultery lies just a squeal away from the bed of swine.[46]

More importantly, through the sexual embraces of this backwoods Lothario, who teaches her more about sex than Reno ever did or could, she is "awakened" for the first time as an amorous woman. Hitherto her relationship with Reno had been coolly tolerant and friendly; all this rutting along the pig traces becomes her *felix culpa*, enabling her later to be more loving as a wife and, presumably, making her marriage more stable. Leafy does, however, learn from her mistakes that the sexual act does not constitute love in the true sense and that, if Cashie can embrace her so readily, he can do so with almost any woman.[47]

Having thus compromised her heroine, the author now begins to keep a balance sheet as if determined that Yanders, who had pilfered a kiss from the girl, and Cashie, who had enjoyed her sexual favors, must now pay a token to the piper. All this helps to tighten the plot, though perhaps too expertly for some tastes. The cuckolded Reno, back at Whitewater, shows for once his mettle by galloping out to search for his wife despite his dangerously infected foot. The foot symbolism here is of lame Vulcan, whose wife Venus was proverbially inconstant. Reno almost kills himself in the derring-do, but he is rescued by Sheriff Yanders, whom Leafy's little brother Offie had freed from the barn; and Reno finally rides to Cincinnati stretched out in Cashie's own wagon, one generously loaned by the seducer for the purpose—yes, he even lies in the very feathered bed his wife had warmed more than once in dalliance.

While we learn these things, the baby continues to show a Tristram Shandy reluctance in getting born. And Leafy's brother, Chancellor, discovers that his life's calling is to be a preacher. Like other figures in the story, he "finds" his identity; and, like others, he has enough difficulties scattered in his path to create reader suspense. A major difficulty for him is Bass, his heavy-handed father, whose Quaker religious thinking is imbued with the darker hues of Calvinism. Bass teaches his boy to keep any acting or preaching talents he might own hidden under a bushel basket, to exaggerate his humility, and to practice self-abasement even at the risk of destroying career initiative. Fortunately, Chancellor is un-cowed by his father. Were he not so proud, confident, and persis-tent, his girlfriend, Venese, an individualist in her own right, would never have been attracted to him.

Venese is well sketched, and the sensual love she stands for paral-lels what happens to Leafy; even so, we cannot help thinking that one of her functions is to add spice to the Blue Grass phase of the story. This rural beauty whets her appetite for meeting Chancellor by encouraging delayed absences, by putting up temporary barriers to their love. And he, Chancellor, enjoys the "chanceyness" (the author's word)[48] of these sylvan encounters, all save the one at which she has daringly arranged to be found naked in the presence of a rival suitor—an act highly improbable even for a teaser. This com-promising exhibition of herself to a man she does not love, followed by the jealousy of her rightful partner, parallels Leafy's surrender to Cashie and Reno's jealously when he learns of her affair. The exhibition in the woods is also sensational for another reason. We see here a rare instance in the West corpus of a detailed physical combat between men, proving that the pacifist author of *Friendly Persuasion* can handle a fight scene when she wants to.

Venese, who likes to woo secluded in a bower of fox grapes, with the fruit "hanging down for the taking . . . sweet and tangy once you got past their skins" (13), clearly suggests by name, by her ren-dezvous, by her mode of pleasure the role of Venus. By every en-dowment she is well fitted to keep a love affair, or a marriage, from growing monotonous. Of all the West heroines she comes closest to deserving the tribute that Shakespeare's Enobarbus pays to Cleopatra: "Age cannot wither her, nor custom stale / Her infinite variety. . . . " Still, Venese is no deceitful adventuress but a back-woods belle practicing on the heart of only one lad. That she is at-tracted to a fellow about to don the sober garb of the ministry may make some readers skeptical. But, ever since Hawthorne's Arthur Dimnesdale of *The Scarlet Letter*, the reading public has been dis-covering that preachers are also human. Bernard De Voto in his *Mark Twain's America* tells of the sexual freedom of the frontier and of the correlation between camp meetings and the marriages that followed for three months afterward. In the light of history, Venese and Chancellor are not, therefore, unusual in their habits.

Miss West manages much of this affair with unwonted discretion, proceeding more by symbols than by such naturalistic detail as attends the Leafy-Cashie liaison. She evidently does not want us to see anything comparable to Sinclair Lewis' Elmer Gantry in Chancellor—he is too goodhearted and too serious for that—yet he is not cautious, prudish, or unvirile. His religious profession should come as no surprise to anyone, for the frontier church in early America offered one of the few opportunities a young man could have for the exercise of power and influence. Like Le Cid in Miss West's *A Matter of Time*, he is free in his love but not loose. Yet we are led to suppose that he and his girlfriend will soon abandon their little prayer meetings in the grape bower, for he tells her that she will have to get herself "saved" just as he did.

In one intriguingly symbolic scene, Chancellor happens upon Venese lying on the school ground one day in the midst of students; her dress is being used as a tablecloth; and she, playing out a game, allows the students to "set" her body with victuals from lunch baskets as if she were a table. Unconsciously aware of erotic significance here—her body is, so to speak, a banquet spread out for the generality—he jerks her to her feet. The implication is that she might give of herself too lightly in other ways unless somehow held in check. After all, her last name is Lucey (loose-y).

In addition to the Chancellor story, there is one about Junius Daubenheyer, a physician who, feeling guilt for the death of his first wife, mourns the past and loses faith in his professional skill until the birth of Leafy's baby and a self-recognition scene with Offie provide the incentive for a change of stance. He is then prepared to love life once more.[49]

When the child is born, Reno believes that Yanders is the father; and he thus participates in one of several ironies found in the final chapters. Cashie is the father, no doubt about it. Consequently, Reno has been doubly deceived. Other ironies break out when various people mistakenly believe that *they* are responsible for the safe delivery; and Leafy permits them to think so though she knows that the major help was Reno's assurance of continued devotion. Because the truth about the paternity is not so explicitly set forth as some readers might desire (some reviewers of the novel surely misunderstood), the following excerpt covering this point is in order: "Everybody here tonight but Reno himself, who said the words I [Leafy] had to hear, ready to claim the credit for what those October nights along the trace produced" (302).

Among the arresting features of the novel must be counted the various double names and name changes. Cashie Wade is also known as Olin; he is dissatisfied with both names; by extension, he is dissatisfied with both of his selves; and he wants to get a new name. Leafy, who turns over a new leaf at the end of the story, is for once able to make up her mind and demands to be known as Mary Pratt. Offie matures enough to want to be called Howard. Prill, the mother, who also undergoes some change in the story, is sometimes called by her girlhood name, Aprilla. Even the doctor has another name, June; and his change of heart has already been mentioned. Reno and Bass neither look for a change in themselves nor make one; their names, accordingly, are fixed. Chancellor, more so the master of himself than the other figures, has no desire to be called anything else.[50]

Jessamyn West takes Realism to greater lengths in *Leafy Rivers* than is usual for her. It is almost as if she were trying harder than ever to purge herself of the reputation of being the author of sweet, charming, innocent Quakerism of the "theeing" and "thouing" variety. For instance, Leafy's family, aptly named the Converses, are of quite another variety than the Birdwells. As Quakers, they have no characteristic manner of speech or dress, voice no pacifist convictions, avoid no physical conflict, and undergo no persecutions as a religious group or even speak of them. Like the Baptists, they attend evangelist camp meetings of the "holy-roller" vintage. (Protestant groups on the early American frontier often became fundamentalist and revivalist, no matter what their original denomination; one reason for this similarity is owing to their common use of meeting facilities, which happens to be the case in *Leafy Rivers*.) Nowhere in the book is there a single instance of the traditional Quaker silent worship. The quaintness is so washed out of *these* Quakers that they might as well have been Lutherans or Presbyterians.

Today, we can hardly claim originality for the theme of a wife's sexual awakening by proxy, especially as pulp novels have elaborated on this subject for decades. Yet Miss West in this instance was probably not catering to a strictly popular market, for there are too many subtleties in the novel to suit the *hoi polloi*. What saves the work from utter mediocrity is this very cleverness.

Regrettably, the writer did not endow Leafy with that richness of humanity making Lib Conboy and Cress Delahanty so live in their books that one truly cares what happens to them. It is true that Miss

West does not have to admire her figures in order to portray them well; but such admiration does seem to help, at least with the leading characters in the longer works. Leafy, throughout, is always kept at arm's length, as if she were an insect being studied out of curiosity; she is a creature apart despite the stream-of-consciousness technique used to reveal her thoughts. In short, she does not engage the author's deepest sympathies—consequently, she does not appeal to the reader's.

Most of the burden in *Leafy Rivers* is carried by technical skill: the clever symbols, the parallelisms, the multiple and interlocking plots which are smoothly resolved. The novel gives the effect of a tour de force, calculated and brilliant, cerebral rather than emotionally appealing. For Jessamyn West probably made the wrong choice of theme *and* heroine. Whatever the cause may be, *Leafy Rivers* somehow does not have the inspired creativity found in certain other of her books.

The ending is so "professional," as Joan Joffe Hall objects in *Saturday Review* (October 7, 1967), that it suggests the influence of formula writing, though Miss Hall does not go so far as to say that. "It's 'professional' in a bad sense too," she continues, "for she strains to tie up loose threads in a tidy ending" (45). That is, for the sake of verisimilitude the ragged edges of life should have been left intact. Moreover, the Hollywood scriptwriting experiences may have proved on this occasion to be a bit too effective. On the other hand, Miss West claims that she saw herself, through having been questioned on her methods by Robert Wyler and his brother William, develop "better ways of telling a story. . . ."[51]

The screenplay writing gave her a marked feeling of gratification in that she was writing for an immediate and appreciative audience (the director and his assistants) and got an immediate response quite unlike the case with published works. Nevertheless, as she reports in *To See the Dream*, the Hollywood stint made her feel a little uneasy in that she might "in time be willing to sacrifice virtues in the writing in return for the warmth of 'working with'. . ." (178). It could be true that, for the sake of this one book, *Leafy Rivers*, she was willing to sacrifice virtues in technique in return for the security of the formula method that is all too common in motion-picture work. Of course, there is also the possibility that she novel was designed for adaptation to the film media. She herself says somewhere in *To See the Dream* that there is a consolation in knowing that what has succeeded before in films may well succeed again. She is without doubt familiar with the clichés; she even used some of them in the *Friendly Persuasion* screenplay. Her several stays in Hollywood could and probably did make her more susceptible than ever to using clichés in her published writings. Indeed, some of the characteristics of the film formula are only too evident in *Leafy Rivers*: each of the major characters has a problem that is resolved at the end; the setting is interestingly different; there is at least a little physical action, even violence which goes counter to her usual practice; raw sex is present; there are two parallel love plots, one to interest married people and the other to interest the younger ones; the "villains" are finally made to pay or to reform a little; and the values of true love and marital fidelity are, in the end, reaffirmed.

CHAPTER 3

In the Land Where Lemons Bloom

THE second and equally important regional background for the literary development of Jessamyn West is California, represented, for the most part, by some science fiction; by two loose collections of short stories, *Love Death and the Ladies' Drill Team* and *Crimson Ramblers of the World, Farewell*; by a unified collection of short stories, *Cress Delahanty*; and by two novels, *South of the Angels* and *A Matter of Time*.

When Miss West had finished with ancestral accounts, which had stimulated her creativity, and gotten Indiana out of her system —save for the belated and only partly Hoosier setting of *Leafy Rivers*[1]—she moved with the California books to the time and experiences commensurate with her own youth. In a way, the shift entailed a challenge. One question was whether she could handle in an extended narrative form, objectively and without morbid overtones, experiences similar to those she had observed or undergone, or could readily imagine doing so, in those years uncomfortably close to her long illness. And whether, if she became personal, she could avoid self-pity. We may state here and now that she succeeded in both respects.

Just as we found that *Friendly Persuasion* had its "corrective" in *Witch Diggers*, which attempted to tell about another aspect of those Indianians who had seemed just a bit too prosperous and happy, so the chaste and proper *Cress Delahanty*, whose heroine is at best only beginning to be aware of the sordid aspects of sex, is followed by the earthy and even bawdy *South of the Angels*, which has an equivalent time and setting. Furthermore, the Quaker church—disguised under another name in *A Matter of Time*—has a diminished role in the moral life of the people, even less than in *Leafy Rivers*. What Tom Mount does with his girlfriends on the floor of the church would be almost unthinkable for the dignified Grove Meeting House mentioned in *Friendly Persuasion*!

I *Fantasies*

Two fantasies showing the California locale deserve special mention, especially *The Pismire Plan* (1948).[2] The latter, unusual for science fiction in being a brilliant satire about the tastelessness and vulgarity of twentieth-century American civilization, came out in the same year that did Evelyn Waugh's *The Loved One*, a satire on the mortuary burial customs in Hollywood. What is offered in the West book is a Brave New World of the absurd. It is a pity that this story is out of print and not generally available to the reading public, for it almost alone of Miss West's inventions reveals her command of burlesque.

George Pismire, whose offensive name suggests antlike efficiency, is a successful Eastern businessman. Driving along the cluttered and overly huckstered California highways, he has shocking encounters along the way: a store that inflicts on each customer a singing commercial, a motel that insists on supplying chargeable items, a Nubian goat raiser who will not sell even a sip of milk unless it be in a vessel made by his crony in the tie-in pottery next door, a cafe catering to luxury dogs, and other places only too reminiscent of actuality. The step-by-step narration of how Pismire arrives at his plan for recompensing the distressed consumer of such vendibles and services—not the dogs, of course, but the human beings—is drolly suspenseful.

Among the profusion of targets for satire are abbreviated company names (A.R.S., for example), the foolishness of Americans who repeat slogans and follow the ratings of this and that product, fancy cemeteries (Isle of the Departed being an open dig at the notorious Forest Lawn), radio and billboard advertising with all its sex madness and grotesquerie, wildly exotic products ("Tasty Rattlesnake Tenderloins"), soap operas, insufferably infantile motion pictures, do-it-yourself establishments, Hollywood footprints set in cement (this time, it is lips), and even psychic fakes—a specialty in California. When Pismire sees a long column of motionless people clinging to a copper wire, some of them throwing a fit once in a while, he is told they are receiving the Hosmer Ripples, which are supposed to be beneficial emanations originating in one mysterious Hosmer Wright to be found in a bungalow at the other end of the wire. The people do not pay for the Ripples, for that would be illegal; instead, they make "love gifts." Out of curiosity, Pismire visits the bungalow and finds the wire tied to nothing more than a stove; Hosmer Wright, who is seated nearby, is contemptuous of the whole gullible crowd; and he is enjoying himself with cowboy and "girlie" magazines.

In due course the outraged Pismire establishes a vast new business called Rent-a-Patron Service whereby selected groups of people, instead of having to endure and be victimized by such things as stupid motion pictures, insipid cafe meals (the dogs get better service), and deadly commercials, are *paid* to test these beforehand. This way, no matter how bad the product, there will always be some consumers for it, if only the testers; and, regardless of how horribly these consumers suffer, they will at least be recompensed for their trouble. The ultimate goal in this mock-serious story is decidedly Huxleyan in that human genes are made to undergo some kind of mutation to insure the birth of the ideal consumer. Since advertising and commerce are so hopelessly bad, the merciful thing is to create people who would not mind them.

In the final ironic scene in this story so studded with ironies, Pismire, at the pinnacle of his success as benefactor to mankind, not to mention businessmen, weeps with joy—"for those generations to come who need never again experience the suffering which had been so common before The Pismire Plan: the suffering of men with uncertain Aptitudes enduring without Recompense an unstable, horrendous way of life. All that was to be changed. Children would be born not only with Stable Aptitudes [is Miss West punning on *stable*?] but with Aptitudes well suited to the environment which awaited them" (95). Only at the very end is the reader reminded of Huxley's 1932 masterpiece, *Brave New World*

What cataclysmic changes would occur in the world if we awakened some morning to find that children had suddenly grown to adult size and that adults, except for a favored few, had all shrunk to the helplessness of dolls? Would the children, by virtue of their now superior stature, obey a natural impulse to dominate their elders and rule mankind? They rule with astonishing results in *The Chilekings* (1967), which depicts a utopia influenced by Wordsworthian views about the innate goodness of children.[3]

An imaginary editor annotates the report of a long-winded, utterly conventional army tank officer named Captain Phipps, a report frequently digressive because it was written by a doddering old man sixty years after the principal events had taken place. In

doleful disillusionment he writes that children destroyed war mu-
nitions everywhere because they had been horrified by the sight of
bloodshed, enthroned a reign of peace, extirpated the profit system,
distributed the goods of the earth equitably, eliminated universal
education, and reversed the sequence whereby the first part of life
had been spent in study and the last part in work. Freudianism
entered, too, in the form of publicized meetings for child-sex activities—innocent and not-so-innocent libidinal play.

Through the use of fantasy, the pacifism of *Friendly Persuasion*
and the adolescent insight of *Cress Delahanty* are thoughtfully used
to treat far-ranging societal issues of significance; but the treatment
is tempered occasionally with wholesome laughter. Something of
the insouciance and exuberance of Pismire is, somewhat to our
disappointment, missing in *The Chilekings*; for the whole scheme is
more consciously worked out, more sophisticated; and the narration
is modeled to the tedious thought patterns of Captain Phipps for
greater psychological realism. *The Chilekings* represents a technical
advance over *Pismire*; yet there must be some readers who prefer
the other fantasy if only because of its freshness and outrageous
mirth.

Writing science fiction is easy for Jessamyn West, although she
is understandably wary that what can be done easily may not be
done well. Assuredly, the best of her longer works are the fruit of
years of patient composing and, in three instances, of reworking
stories into integrated patterns.

II *Mysteries of Life Made Orderly*

Love Death and the Ladies' Drill Team, stories published in the
journals over a period of seventeen years, came out in 1955.[4] Naming the book after its title story proved most apt, as many of the
stories do deal with love or death in some manner. Among the
preponderantly favorable reviews of this first West collection of her
ununified items was one by Carlos Baker in the *New York Times
Book Review*. Following a passage in which he praises her for com-
bining so well the ironic, the pathetic, and the curious, he avers
that "The Mysteries of Life in an Orderly Manner" is the one story
in the group which best describes Miss West's aims in writing.[5]
Baker is acute in this observation, for Miss West does find in even
the most commonplace events a mystery worth communicating;
and she communicates not in the tortured style of a William Faulk-

ner or a Franz Kafka, who hint at a universe too complex for simple explanation, but in the orderly manner of a rich and mature mind that has, for better or worse, escaped becoming demon ridden. Beethoven may have needed his storm and lightning flash, but Bach did wonders with calm weather.

Emily Cooper, who figures in two of the stories, first shows up in "The Mysteries of Life in an Orderly Manner." This piece resembles many being written today insofar as it treats a revelation of character or the exploration of a situation as its main goal, rather than a physical adventure or a problem to be solved. When Mr. Cooper drives his wife into the California hill town on initiation night so that she can at last join the Pocahontas Lodge, he subjects her reverence for ceremony and rule to a dose of good-natured levity. For instance, as they wait in the parked car, Emily happens to object to some passing members carrying candles to the meeting because, as she articulates in the approved parlance of the true follower, "The lodge treats of the mysteries of life in an orderly manner," but candles are not part of that order. To which Mr. Cooper makes the mistake of responding, "Maybe they are part of the mystery."[6]

He is nevertheless the norm in the story, for he can see the joiner instinct in its absurd aspect and yet remain sufficiently tolerant. Emily's weakness, like that of many converts to secret organizations, is that she lacks a sense of humor which might enable her to see the arcana of titles, rituals, and regalia from the point of view of the skeptical outsider. She takes everything too seriously ("Don't joke about serious things," she tells him angrily).

But the meaning runs still deeper. Various passages in the dialogue suggest that the real reason Emily is joining the lodge is her lack of confidence in herself; at least, her husband will not supply it to her ("You don't give me any confidence"), whereas the close fellowship found in the organization might provide just what she needs, or make her think it does so if only by supplying a factitious sense of order among the mysteries of her world. The success of the story is partly achieved by the fine balance maintained between Emily's viewpoint and that of her husband; there is some justice on both sides. The Coopers seem to have a poor marriage, and Emily accordingly needs something which her husband, the self-sufficient and self-confident one, cannot or will not provide her.

In "Love, Death, and the Ladies' Drill Team" we see her on a

September day within the Pocahontas circle and looking out upon what she has somehow missed. The scene is an upstairs room, Burnham Hall, which is used by the lodge for their weight-reducing and figure-enhancing exercises. Emily Cooper is now thirty-six, her children are in school, and her empty house has spoken to her of middle-aged loneliness; hence, the lodge is now a drill master enabling her to endure, in a kind of passionless stoicism, the long and loveless glide into old age and death. For all the bored, overweight, unloved, and unloving women, the lodge is now a substitute husband.

As Emily sits by a window in the hall waiting for Mrs. Rotunda (delightful name!) to get the drill started, she and other matrons notice below in a vacant lot a female called Imola standing in the wind, shortly to be joined by her lover, Ramos. The two below, described in sensual terms, represent the very freedom, passion, and love which the individual females in the drill team lack. Therefore, when Mrs. Tetford pities Imola, she is unconsciously ironic; but Emily knows that *pity* is not called for.

The wind, as Christopher G. Katope points out in an explication of the story,[7] is definitely important in unifying the structure; nevertheless, contrary to what he says, it does not signalize any "renewed vitality" in the protagonist. If Emily goes beyond the observing stage to learn a lesson, the story does not imply it. To be sure, she imagines that she is "the one responsive and harmonious harp" that feels the force of the September wind; yet, Katope's interpretation notwithstanding, she does not transcend this feeling into resolve and action. In Percy B. Shelley's "Ode to the West Wind," the Romantic analogue to which Katope refers, the *persona* does pass into resolve and action; in the case of Emily, sad to say, no change takes place. Miss West hints at the analogue for the purpose of irony. The wind, symbolic of passion, blows everywhere, around the spindly legs of merchants on the street, and among blue dust flowers in the lot—but not in the hall.

Images of love and death abound in the work. The sexual aspects of love show in the description of Imola, whose dress blows against her thighs; who wears no brassiere; who is said to sunbathe in the nude with guitar-playing Ramos. Their kisses down in the lot are enough to throw all the staring ladies into bemused silence. Death is suggested by Emily's thoughts on aging, the sight of the undertaker, the talk about funerals, the presence of a Miss Graves, and

In the Land Where Lemons Bloom

other things not quite so direct, such as the description of Mrs. Rotunda's gray hair "arranged with all the finality of marble. . . ."

In "A Time of Learning" the young house painter Emmett Macquire learns what it is like to suffer from unrequited love. One painting of his in the barn at home symbolizes what will happen to him after he goes to work at the farm where pretty Ivy Lish lives. At the Lishes, the youth is put to work painting the barn. Within no time at all, he has fallen in love with the daughter, Ivy; and he is inspired to create a portrait of her that far outshines anything to be expected of a mere barn painter. But little does he know that all his depth of feeling and power of expression are lost on the fickle girl, who thoughtlessly gives the portrait as a gift to one of her suitors. In this type of story which reveals the heartbreak that goes with growing up—tender young love laying its sacrifice on the altar of indifference—the author almost invariably succeeds—and succeeds memorably.

In contrast with this account of the true artist—or at least the artist *pro tempore*—there is the artist *manqué* in the odd "Tom Wolfe's My Name." For years, Mr. Sterling (there is irony in his name; Miss West's stories are filled with charactonyms) has derived unnatural pleasure from pretending to townspeople to be the veritable Thomas Wolfe who is secluded on a California grape orchard in order to escape publicity. There he does all of his "writing," or rather copying, of the Wolfe books into big ledgers that are kept for visitors to see. The narrator, a textbook salesman named Madden, who had always doubted Sterling, chances to read in a newspaper about Wolfe's death in Baltimore and decides that now would be just the right time to pay the pretender a call. At this moment the suspense of wondering how the grape man will explain his being alive begins.

Of course, the main interest for the reader, if not for the salesman, does not consist in proving Sterling a charlatan; the reader has been made dubious enough from the outset. What remains—if this story is to be truly meaningful—is to discover some clue to the hitherto hidden inner life of the impostor. Sterling's ordinarily empty eyes, which change and come to a focus when he introduces himself as Thomas Wolfe, lets us know that he has an *idée fixe* that gives him his principal sense of reality. This clue is, unfortunately, the only one given about his inner life.

Madden finds the study on the ranch to be a jumble of papers,

91

pans, dirty laundry, books, and milk bottles—all the paraphernalia to fit the Wolfe legend. But he is amazed to find Sterling dead on the couch, and next to him is the ledger into which he had been copying Wolfe's *The Story of a Novel*. But nowhere does Madden find a newspaper reporting the death of the novelist. We are supposed to believe, evidently, that Sterling had so completely identified himself with his idol over the years (maybe the liar ultimately believes his own lie?) that his very heartbeat is coexistent with Wolfe's. This trick ending falls a bit flat, despite the interesting story line throughout. The lack of pervasive supernatural foreshadowing, or hint of fate, or other means of reinforcing the idea of the bizarre, makes us wait in vain to hear the other shoe drop. The death should have been rationally or supernaturally explained; either one or a combination of these.

We might argue that Wolfe's *The Story of a Novel* is fairly short, is only a pamphlet, and that its publication two years before the real author's demise would have allowed an enterprising fraud like Sterling to have copied it earlier. Another minor flaw in the story is that Wolfe's use of ledgers for producing manuscripts was restricted to the *Wanderjahr* period when the first draft of *Look Homeward Angel* was written, and was abandoned after that except for keeping notes and travel jottings.[8] Probably Miss West was appealing to the popular conception then held by the public. In any case, "Tom Wolfe's My Name" is one of her infrequent stories of the fantastic. Her skill in this genre is not a mean one, as we have noted in discussing her science fiction. Otherwise, fantasy is hardly her *métier*.

"Foot-Shaped Shoes" recalls the idyllic early period of the author in Hemet just after graduation from Whittier. Its hero is a big, strapping adolescent named Rusty, who is modeled after her brother Merle West (the book's dedication reads: "For Merle—Rusty grown up"). Such predisposition being the case, it is no wonder that Rusty's sister is a young newlywed who adores her brother about as much as she does her husband. The best-drawn figure in the story is the heartless whore, Mrs. Campos, who is so contemptible in the treatment of her son that the reader can find in her very little kinship with the endearing strumpets of John Steinbeck's *Sweet Thursday*. The existence of Mrs. Campos proves that Miss West can portray evil in its repellent aspects when she so desires. For the most part, the story is iridescent with happy sentiment about the newlyweds' adoption of the Campos boy.

Harrison Smith's review of *Love Death and the Ladies' Drill Team* in the December 3, 1955, issue of *Saturday Review* tremendously underestimated one of the best sketched of all the West villains, "Horace Chooney, M.D." Contrary to the reviewer's statement, Chooney is not "an elderly and humane doctor," is not suffering from an ailment soon to kill him, and does not have a benign attitude toward his female patient, who is not an adolescent but a lady of twenty-two or twenty-three. We can see in this review how the reputation of the sweet and charming Quaker author— the *gentle* author, too, who brought innocent little Cress into the world—has caused misinterpretation. The story of Chooney is really about a cultivated but cruel, sensual physician, who, having had some affair in the city with a lady patient who had died (though she was normal at the outset of treatment), finds it suddenly necessary to abscond to the country and to assume a new name in order to escape notoriety and perhaps to rebuild a practice.

Miss Chester, his most recent victim, whom he finds physically attractive—something of the lamb for the tiger in him to victimize, because he delights in testing his power to hurt and wound—has no serious ailment aside from mere loneliness. Without giving a fig for the Hippocratic oath, Chooney makes her case seem serious, deludes her with a few photographs of the woman he has ruined, and discreetly makes an appointment to commence his diabolic treatment. Chooney, in short, is a sadistic sensualist, an emotional vampire of a particularly corrupting species.[9]

"Dr. Chooney, M.D." is as carefully wrought as any of the short works of Faulkner or Hemingway. It is full of irony, that holy grail sought after by today's literary explicators, especially in the scene where Chooney manipulates the photographs. Not the least of the ironies is, as Miss West herself observed, that *Mademoiselle* magazine first brought to light the malpractices of this medical bluebeard.

Just as the villains of Katherine Mansfield are tagged as thoughtless, animallike extroverts; those of Willa Cather as snobs and materialists; those of Edith Wharton as fashionable, immoral hypocrites; those of Jessamyn West reveal a foolish ignorance of external nature or are symbolically related to nature's cruel or perverted features. Mary Abel disfigures the earth with diggings and burns pigs; Dr. Chooney watches with pleasure a woodpecker devouring his prey; Tom Mount, too occupied with carnal quests in *South of the Angels*, cannot tell a buzzard from a hawk; Mr. Wallenius (*Cress Delahanty*) drowns snakes for the fun of it; "Senator" Whitehall ("The Battle of the Suits") hates bees even though they once saved his life; and Mrs. Prosper, in the next story to be considered, tells the singing birds outside her window they are fools, regrets not having seen a certain monkey drown, and is the proud owner of a cat whose specialty is biting flies.

The version of "A Little Collar for the Monkey" in the collection is an improvement over the one published in *Woman's Home Companion* in February, 1948; it contains additional concrete, descriptive details, and the imagery is more vivid. As a rule, Miss West improves her short stories before publishing them in collections if there is a long time lapse. This improvement is more thorough than just restoring the cuttings that magazine publication might have required.

Mrs. Prosper of "A Little Collar for the Monkey" is afflicted with Dr. Chooney's moral ailment of a perverted intelligence that seeks to gratify itself in a cruel lust for power over a helpless female; she wants to rule absolutely her marriageable daughter Lily. One of Mrs. Prosper's recreations had been to keep a sturdy apricot tree in her yard from bearing fruit by breaking off all the buds each spring. Maybe she will continue to keep Lily sterile, too, she thinks, by driving away all suitors. But, on the morning the story opens, a fish peddler intends to outwit the mother and to elope with the long-suffering Lily. On the way to learning the denouement, the reader discovers one of the richest of all the West stories as regards character contrast.

"Home-Coming" studies the problem a newly released sanatorium patient has in trying to adjust his own enfeebled constitution to the robust pace of his wife. Having been drained of his strength by trying to please the selfish woman, he gropes his way back to the sanatorium within just a few hours, lucky to be still alive. The setting much resembles La Viña Sanatorium. Compared with the other pieces in the book, "Home-Coming" is, however, a tour de force. Miss West's pieces about sanatorium and valetudinarian life do not, as a rule, rank among her very best, and not simply because the subject of disease is of indifferent interest among the well. Her essential spirit, as witnessed in many a story, is a youthful, ardent response to living, to just being alive.

Leonard Hobart in "Public-Address System" ends in another

kind of sanatorium, a mental hospital. This selection begins in a manner unusual for Miss West—at the end of the story. Then, after capturing the reader's interest about why Bill Hare is currently unpopular in town, she reverts to his first association with the potential lunatic, Leonard, and starts to work forward. The opening of "Public-Address System" has about it the slickness of the popular magazine where formulas are rampant. But, as soon as we break past the opening and become acquainted with Leonard Hobart's incipient irrationality, the cause of his long silence over the years, and finally his emergence into speechified thunder as a sports announcer, we find it difficult to lay the story down.

The final two selections which we shall examine here are about adolescents in institutions. Doubtless the author's actual experience as a teacher and as the wife of a teacher and school administrator accounts for much of the Realistic school atmosphere. Harry "Senator" Whitehall, the fifteen-year-old brat who struts through "The Battle of the Suits," should be evidence enough for anyone who missed the mindless spite in "The Ouija Board," wherein a little girl consumed with hatred for her mother favors an adulterous union between her father and a female relative, that Miss West can and does invent some unsavory young people. The story of the "Senator" is told from the point of view of a janitor named Joe Ortiz, employed in the Temple Home for Boys. Ortiz' mistake is to have bought for himself a double-breasted, pin-striped suit identical to one later purchased by the "Senator." Naturally, the feelings of the pompous and self-pitying youngster are too important to permit a mere janitor to be seen with such a suit on, and he protests to the superintendent. In the battle of the suits, Joe refuses to take his garments back to the store for a refund. The all-too-familiar atmosphere of the "progressive," student-oriented school system prevails here.

A mildly sarcastic tone appears in some of the ludicrous passages, such as the one in which Joe reflects that his tormentor once had his life saved by being fed diluted honey: "He [Joe] had studied classic myths at San Miguel High School, and he had an unpleasant picture now of the Senator, a big, fat, black-haired baby, being suckled by an oversize, hairy-legged bee. Maybe there would be a statue of it on the courthouse lawn someday" (62). And again, when Joe counters the superintendent's claim that the "Senator" has had a "rough life . . . underprivileged up to now": " 'I know,' Joe said.

'He was brought up by the bees' " (66).

Every now and then some author writes a narrative that is wonderfully heartwarming and is seemingly derived from some Wordsworthian remembered experience, or maybe imagined in some state of inspired euphoria. Dylan Thomas' "A Child's Christmas in Wales" is a fair specimen; Theodor Storm's *Immensee* is another. And such a story is Jessamyn West's "The Singing Lesson" which contains the incomparable piano tuner, Wilbur Smiley, who one day appears at Miss McManaman's country school and treats them all to a medley of song. Upon his entrance, he shocks the teacher with a vulgar simile, but he soon endears himself with his bluff, unconventional wisdom. The following dialogue gives us an idea of his personality; it also illustrates a gift that Miss West has for originating colloquial speech of an amusing turn for her tradesman or lower-class figures:

> "Please," began Miss McManaman again. "To whom . . . ?"
> "Wilbur Smiley, Smiley by name but damned melancholy by nature."
> "You musn't . . ."
> " 'You musn't swear, Mr. Smiley, before the dear little children.' "
> "Well, you musn't," she said.
> "Paugh," said Mr. Smiley. "Where'd you learn the bad words you know, Miss? Right here," he said pointing.
> "In the boys. *And* the girls. . . . What's the worst you know, children?"
> A dozen hands went up.
> "Ta ta, children," he reproved them.
> "You see?" he asked Miss McManaman. "It's in 'em. Working like yeast in a barrel and frothing at the bunghole. Treat 'em like human beings," he advised. "Or cure 'em if you're a mind to. Make 'em spend a day writing bad words on the blackboard. That'll take the brimstone out of them." (238-39)

Having delivered himself of these startling *obiter dicta*, he flattens her by saying that tuning the school piano would be a sheer waste of money since only she, the teacher, ever plays it. The school woodbox, with its pet ground owl and semidrowned squirrels and family of field mice, provokes another jocularity from him: "What's this? . . . Fur-bearing wood [?] "

The classroom is besieged from without by steadily falling rain and saved from its regular lesson by this vital rough who has come among them to judge everything from his own bluff perspective. It seems a warm and homey place now. Smiley is decidedly raw and novel, although honest, in the teacher's eyes: maybe he is not objectionable. Learning that he had interrupted their singing lesson, he suddenly decides that he will sing to them himself. From this sad-faced little man with the peaked head and deep-sunken eyes pours a stream of delicious melody that wafts Miss McManaman off in a rapture of bliss and pain: "As if all the things of which she had dreamed and for which she had waited, without having a name for them, were now spread before her, named, shining, and palpable . . . also that they would vanish: melt, run away, be lost forever. And that was pain" (241). As ironic counterpoint, Smiley has his own love sorrow; and this sorrow explains why his song is poignant: Smiley, the nightingale, has a thorn in his throat. Jessamyn West has woven a mood and a spell with the hauntingly beautiful effect that we find in, for instance, Saroyan's play *My Heart's in the Highlands*, where the old pauper MacGregor moves everyone with the playing of his bugle.

At the close, when Smiley leaves, it is as if some never-to-be-recovered enchantment goes with him into the sullen day and over whatever rainbow bridge supposedly connects the mundane world with the aerial reaches of art. Thoughtfully, he has left behind him a legacy of encouragement for a teacher who cannot sing—"You've got grace notes in your eyes, Mary, and whole ballads in your hands" (248)—and some songs for the class to practice. Mr. Smiley reminds us a trifle of Professor Quigley with respect to his musical talent and crisp readiness of tongue, yet he is assuredly a unique, fully realized, and unforgettable personality.

III *Beautiful Youth*

Judging from current tastes, an assured way for the writer of adolescent fiction to survive is to use the child to comment upon the adult world, as in Twain's *The Adventures of Huckleberry Finn*, Salinger's *The Catcher in the Rye*, and Golding's *Lord of the Flies*; for the reaction seemingly indicates that interest in childhood for its own sake is not enough to please adult readers. Such books enjoy today a somewhat greater popularity than do Booth Tarkington's *Seventeen* and Stratton-Porter's *A Girl of the Limberlost*, which are largely devoid of serious overtones. Miss West's *Cress Delahanty*, as we shall see later in this study, does have a few serious overtones that reflect not so much on adult life, however, as on the universal problems of growing up. Its present popularity (it has been a Book-of-the-Month-Club selection), coupled with substantial intrinsic merit, may well be enough to keep it above the welter of books on childhood that reach the market these days.[10] This volume contains some of the choicest writing of Miss West.

Just as her beloved Thoreau had done in *Walden*, Miss West organizes her book into an ostensible chronology; she uses the seasons to mark time, and she treats only a limited period in the youth of the principal figure. But otherwise there is, of course, little correlation between their methods. The five parts of the story collection—too loosely constructed to be a novel—handle Cress's years from twelve to sixteen; within these parts, the chapters are titled by the various seasons: "Summer I," "Summer II," and so forth. The process of unifying the once disparate stories into a whole is more successful than it is in *Friendly Persuasion*, doubtless because of the close attention paid to chronology.

The earliest story, thus assimilated and renamed, constitutes the opening; "The Child's Day" (1940) stars the elfin figure Minta Eilertson. A few years later Cress Delahanty showed up in the magazine stories along with Chapple Norby. In the late 1940's and 1950's, diminutive heroines for other parts of the future book sprang into serial print as Kate Kinsman, Connie Malloy, and Virginia Hanrahan, Irish lasses most of them. Somehow the author selected the tall, big-boned, tow-headed Cress Delahanty to embody all their separate personalities and adventures in growing up, whether idealized ones from biography or purely invented ones.

In the book, Crescent Delahanty is first disclosed as a quaintly dreamy adolescent who is attitudinizing poetically all alone one October day when her parents, John and Gertrude, have gone for a drive. As subsequent descriptions show, the ranch and the nearby town of Tenant (a mythical town recurring in several West books) much resemble Yorba Linda; and Cress herself seems a little Jessamyn West. The exquisiteness of the opening section is difficult to translate into plot summary; for it is a series of smoothly shifting impressions of what it is like to be a twelve-year-old lass, sensitive, loveable, boy crazy. But Cress is also intelligent, is enjoying being alone with her notebook of Shelleyan phrases, her book of private poems, her plain nourishing lunch of cocoa-sugar-milk paste, the wind which murmurs without, and the cheerful flames crackling in the fireplace. The atmosphere is delightfully cozy.

In Cress's ingenuous comments to herself, we see the first hints of puberty. And, true to the condition of childhood, feeling and wondering, not reasoning, are the paramount states of mind. Despite Cress's fascination with vocabulary, she is yet unable to articulate in speech what she sees of herself in the mirror, she stripped of underclothing and attired in nothing but her mother's black lace shawl. Consequently, she dances the word: "She danced it until she trembled and leaning on bent elbows looked deep into the mirror and said, 'There is nothing I will not touch. I am Cress. I will know everything' " (26). This passage well miniaturizes not only the daydreaming propensity of the young but the flexibility of the art of dancing to express feelings incommunicable in words. It is often risky to engage in biographical criticism; still, we suspect that on one level of interpretation Cress can be considered the *persona* for the novice writer in Jessamyn, whose vow back around 1940 might have been: "I will not be denied any insight into human nature. In the sphere of writing, I will attempt everything someday, will not be a Play Safe Compromiser afraid that neighbors and friends in the community where I live may recognize in my books portraits of themselves.[11] Let the Grundys and the Quakers take their chances, too, for the saying runs, whoever chooses to serve goodness rather than truth, or both simultaneously, is in danger of serving neither." However, Cress does not aspire to authorship nor does she do anything that would shock today's readers even though she dares enough to keep them interested.

Next she is at high school evincing her interest in boys by befriending, a little too vigorously, the shy and bespectacled Edwin Kibbler. At that time she unintentionally shatters an olla, the falling fragments of which knock out some of his teeth; but all ends well, for she becomes his girlfriend. In *South of the Angels*, a love affair begins in a similar way.

After her beloved Grandmother dies, Cress goes to cook for and comfort Grandfather. At first, she believes that his drinking and his arguing with his crony, Mr. Powers, prove he lacks feeling for his dead wife. The wise Powers takes her aside and assures her that appearances are deceiving, that the old man is hurt too profoundly to give his sorrow mere verbal expression. At hearing this correction, Cress stiffens; nonetheless, the lesson sinks home, and she comes to a fuller understanding of human nature. A lesser artist than Miss West would at this point perhaps have Cress break down in tears or run off to Grandfather for forgiveness. But Jessamyn

West believes in honing emotion to keenness by indirection and at the same time making it acceptable through restraint. Also here, as elsewhere, she avoids the "switcheroo" or reversal technique that she condemned in *To See the Dream*, whereby the fundamental makeup in a character is altered. What takes place in Cress is development, "becoming more of the same," as the author defines development. "All the best writing," Miss West declared in *To See the Dream*, "has been of those who become more and more themselves, of the discovery by the hero of himself" (146). Cress understands where she has erred.

In an adventure similar to one Miss West had as a girl, Cress at a beach resort drops her gorgeously colored hat into an aquarium where the dyes, to her public embarrassment, so stain the water that her father has to buy all the fish as restitution.[12]

To gain popularity at school she devises Delahanty's Law, which means carrying her shoes to the bus in the morning and putting them on there so that she can save dressing time. True to her intent, this practice gets her talked about; but her notoriety backfires when she applies for the post of freshman editor and finds that no one thinks her serious and responsible enough for the job. It is the lesson Willy Loman in the play *Death of a Salesman* learned too late: do not try to be popular at the expense of the solid virtues.

In "Winter II," we meet Cress's friend Bernardine, the school's most popular girl. Bernardine, who is anything but natural, insists on being called Nedra on Fridays out of respect for a rich young man whom she had said no to once just before he died and left her nothing. Cress, scheduled to perform in a folk dance, is worried that her usual awkwardness might cause her to trip and make an embarrassing blunder. In comparison with this fear now haunting her, Bernardine's artificiality and snobbery become unbearable. Cress learns to know better not merely her friend but herself as a fallible creature, human, afraid.

Another of her lessons in maturing deals with illicit sex. Mrs. Charlesbois keeps unwitting Cress around after piano lessons in order to cover up an affair she is having with an accordian-playing laborer. Suspense mounts after the girl discovers she is being used and tries to enlighten Mr. Charlesbois, who unaccountably forestalls her with evasive pleasantries and a "crooked Jack O'Lantern smile." The shocker arrives on the next to the last page, where the "deceived" husband discloses obliquely that he knows about the intrigue; that he condones it; and that, as she had earlier sensed, he harbors an indecent interest in Cress herself. The story is a masterpiece of innuendo and veiled allusion, whose contents are adequately manifest to the perceptive and yet discreetly inoffensive to any young readers. If there is a strained note anywhere, it has to do with Cress's sucking a lemon after her illumination: a too-obvious symbol of the taste of this experience. Counterbalancing the Charlesbois story and offering an example of innocent young love is the episode about Edwin's rehearsing his Latin in the springtime arroyo while blonde admirer Cress looks on.

"Spring II" finds Cress about to spend the night with Ina Wallenius in her home on the side of Kettle Hill, which resembles in some ways the Olinda of Jessamyn West's girlhood. The "ratty little town," as her schoolmate Ina labels it, consists of small, uniform, company houses shaded by pepper trees from the sight of the many oil derricks rising like warts on the hillside. Added attractions are pumps that never cease throbbing and the ubiquitous fragrance of raw oil. Lurking in this unpleasant scene is the father, a Bible-reading sadist who keeps his daughter slaving at every household chore. He sometimes shows Ina his gratitude by openly arranging a little punishment for some peccadillo of hers. In the climax of the story, the ogre takes Cress for a walk and shows her what jolly sport it is to catch harmless gopher snakes and drown them in the oily sump holes. When one snake struggles in vain to stay afloat, Cress protests it will die. "Maybe so, maybe not," he deliberates coolly. "It's too early to say. Sink—swim; sink—swim . . ." (181-82). More so than with the depiction of odious Mrs. Prosper, another household tyrant, the present one seems to be taken right out of life. But the illusion of actuality can be the measure of art.

"Early Summer," a little concerto played on the theme of loneliness, begins with a sparkling arpeggio speaking of *tempus edax rerum*; and it ends with an organlike diminuendo telling of the hopelessness of unrequited love. Calvin Dean, the star of the school debating squad, does not even know that wistful Cress, now all of fourteen, has a "crush" on him. Miss West's remarkably sensitive prose style, attuned to every nuance of her lovesick adolescent, once more shows what it can accomplish:

> She had more feelings than she knew what to do with, more emotions than her tranquil life permitted her to discharge. She had to invent sor-

rows and concoct dramas. She would stoop down to rejoice with a daf-
fodil that pushed a stone aside in its upward thrust, or would loosen a
butterfly from a spider web with wailings that brought her no sympathy
from any listener. As if she cared for sympathy! She was capable emotionally of a woman's tragedies and, up to now, she had been unable to
overtake any of these. Now, however, she loved and was not loved in
return.(188)

This passage has the authentic ring of youth's emotional plight.
Youth *is* a tortured, emotional chaos for many people; at best it is a
checkered existence. And, where unreciprocated love is concerned,
the sorrow is perhaps impossible to articulate in all its knife-edge
sharpness save by the uncommon writer who himself has suffered
through it all and remembers. Ames, near the end of Theodore Dreiser's novel, tells Carrie Meeber: "Most people are not capable of
voicing their feelings. They depend upon others. That is what genius
is for." And most adults, in reviewing their childhood from the calm
remove of middle age or later, tend to discount its painful side and
to crown the whole experience with a golden halo. But the true artist, for instance a Jessamyn West, penetrates the barrier which adults have erected against their too often anguished youth, where
self-doubt, humiliation, grudge, and deprivation conspire to make
a brief hell on earth, and shows what those bittersweet days were
really like.

We suspect that this section of the book might be especially autobiographical. Dr. Boyce says that Calvin Dean was a real boy, "of
a good family in Fullerton attending the Fullerton schools in Jessamyn's day. Why did she use the real name . . . when all the other
names where fictitious? Was she yielding to a long desire to tell
Calvin that as a girl, she admired him very much?"[13] Miss West, who
has two answers to this explanation, admits having an unfortunate
habit of using names of people she knows. Moreover, she was not
trying to convey anything to Calvin Dean, although he was the
school hero—a "big football player" and president of the student
body—that all the freshman girls, including herself, "worshipped."[14]
We sooner or later learn, however, that the craftsmanship of this
lady from Napa is often steeped in love. *Cress Delahanty*, rather
than being a private love letter to Calvin Dean, is more plausibly
an open one to the world.

In "Summer I" Cress comes to know the poignance of losing a
girlhood friend who grows up and is about to be married, about to

enter that mystique of wifely interests so strangely excluding in the eyes of the uninitiated maiden. "Summer II" shows her at a beach party where she gets her idealism trampled on by vain, empty-headed, and stuffy schoolmates whose unspoken desire is to be on the lookout for boys but who pretend to be shocked when anyone takes an honest and direct approach in mentioning sex. Well pictured are the boorish boy catcher, Yolande, and the depressingly unoriginal twins, Avis and Mavis Davis. So is Aunt Iris, the lame biologist whose misfortune is to be their chaperon and who is first presented in the story as an oddity; in the final pages, she emerges as a fully rounded human being (insofar as possible in a short story containing so many characters). The description of Aunt Iris' bedroom filled with books, magazines, phonograph, and laboratory equipment aptly attests that this woman has been living a full life despite her handicap: "it looked like a place where a person was living, not empty and bare as the girls' rooms were, places where they were only waiting"(235). The chaperon's situation points up to the hollowness that the girls endure, their utter dependence upon external things, upon coming events such as engagement or marriage, to give their lives fulfillment. This woman has not postponed living.

Then there are pimples to make Cress keep all the shades in the Delahanty house pulled down the whole winter. As if this situation were not risible enough, her mother signs her up in a talent contest in which the blonde presents a skit that puzzles everyone. Fortunately, she is mature enough now to criticize herself objectively and to accept failure with such cheer as to mystify her parents all over again.

Cress's platonic love for the dying Mr. Cornelius is told in part through an extended interior monologue, the first and only instance of this technique in the book, but in its way it prepares for the method used later in *A Matter of Time*. Cress has such a selfless adoration for the thirty-eight-year-old Cornelius that she asks the Lord to accept her in his place. This episode is one of those few stories, so states Miss West, which have any basis in her own experience. It has its inspiration in the case of Harold Nixon, Richard Nixon's older brother, who, after considerable suffering, died of tuberculosis. As the author explains, "It somehow became my conviction [as a little girl] that I should offer the Lord my life in return for Harold's. And I did so, in all sincerity, I thought. The Lord, however, preferred Harold. . . ."[15]

Each passing day is for Cornelius, as for the doomed Mary Jessup in *South of the Angels*, bathed in the radiance of eternity. Now that he is about to leave the world, he is sharply sensitive to the delights of sensory impressions—"tipped the cup of seeing until he had the last drop"—almost as if he had perused and taken to heart Walter Pater's concluding advice in *The Renaissance* on the necessity to collect, treasure, and luxuriate in what Pater terms "this fruit of quickened, multiplied consciousness."

The two stories featuring Cornelius, particularly the second one, have all the quality of genuine tenderness, yet are fully controlled through the use of esthetic distance. When the girl goes against the advice of conventional friends to tell the man to his face, but with his wife listening, that she loves him, had even planned to run away with him and nurse him back to health, the reader derives an unwonted pleasure and gratification at witnessing such open honesty.

For the conclusion of the book, Jessamyn West rewrote an item she had published in 1946 in *Harper's* under the title "Grandpa Was Her Mirror." The story is about a girl's redemptive experience in confronting the fact of death and her emergence into womanhood. Probably no more rewarding study can be made of the growth of Jessamyn West as a craftsman than comparing these two versions. Edwin is absent in the original. In lieu of the mother in that version, there is a much older sister, Myra, work-worn but compassionate, whose role as mistress of the household entitles her to take charge of Chapple when Mr. Norby brings the latter home from Woolman College to be at the bedside of dying Grandpa. In both versions, everyone expects the college girl to be cold and indifferent toward the old man; and she is at first. Having rejected the old gardener at Woolman, her initial attitude toward Grandpa comes as no surprise. Hers is almost the same distaste for old men as the young waiter has in Hemingway's "A Clean, Well-Lighted Place": they are uninteresting, repellent, burdensome.

For the book version, Edwin is put on Woolman campus, partly to help round out the structure of the cycle, of course, yet also to point up early in the story how self-centered Cress has become at sixteen and away from home. In this manner, Edwin functions somewhat as the sardonic Myra did in the magazine story, only he loves the girl in the special way that only a boyfriend can and is, therefore, more effectual when he gives her advice. His advice prepares her for her ultimate moment of awareness at the bedside. As indicated earlier, Miss West has no penchant for the trick ending.

The last improvement appears in the passage beginning with Grandpa's remarks about the yellow violets. It is true that now the real Reservoir Hill is substituted for North Hill, yet this is no gain except for pleasing those few readers familiar with Yorba Linda landscape. More certain improvement comes with the elimination of the sentimentality in the original—"Tears filled his faded eyes and spread over the tight skin of his cheek bones."[16] And more still in altering the moral of the story and in making that moral unobtrusive. In the original, Grandpa's farewell to the violets ("Now I have to leave them") causes Chappel to fear that death also can and will come to her, that she is consequently one with the old man as regards sad mortality. When she sobs, she sobs for herself, not especially for him. An ancient and much respected device is the use of fear of death to reform the living.

Cress comes to a richer understanding. She shares something esthetically and emotionally significant with the dying man, despite his age; and this something is their love for the yellow violets, which triggers her sympathy: "You were young [as I am now]," runs the final version as found in the book, "and you loved flowers. . . . And you still do. . . . Just like me"(311). Not their bond in death but their bond in the beauty of life unites them. Cress is lifted then into an awareness of the sympathies that properly unite youth with age.

There is evidence to support Dr. Boyce when he says that *Cress Delahanty* is the "thinly disguised story of her [Jessamyn's] girlhood."[17] Besides the parallels already indicated, the sensitive girl in each instance grows up in a new settlement among the citrus groves about one and a half hours by train from Woolman (patently Whittier), whose route passes through La Habre and then Brea; the seashore is only a short drive away; Saddle Back Mountain and Reservoir Hill are in view; the father is a citrus grower and an officer on the school board; the girl is a freckled tow-head with literary tastes, who has a grandmother who dies; and, in addition to being fond of yellow violets, she attends a Quaker college fairly early and gets on the debating and basketball teams. To summarize, Cress has an environment much like that which Jessamyn West had known, plus some tastes and some experiences which are undeniably similar to the author's. But the book is not deliberate autobiography; on the other hand, the use of autobiographical details adds to the verisimilitude of the work.

The two years spent in reworking and assembling the magazine stories[18] were well spent. Of thirteen reviews of *Cress Delahanty* that could be located, not a single one constitutes what could be called an attack; on the contrary, the general feeling ran quite the other way. Such overwhelming approbation, we fear, is enough to make academia think the book assuredly deficient, for literary scholars almost take it for granted that greatness means neglect; and, to make matters even worse, *Cress Delahanty* has sold well from the beginning.

Miss West's friend Edward Weeks, in his review in *Atlantic* (January, 1954), compared her favorably with Booth Tarkington for peeking "so surely and so sunnily into the adolescent world." Riley Hughes in the *Catholic World* (March, 1954) dubbed the work "exquisite." In the *New York Herald Tribune Book Review* (January 3, 1954), Dan Wickenden, aside from profuse general praise, opined that Miss West was able to illuminate with her own special magic even the most commonplace things. Frances Gaither's coverage in the *New York Times Book Review*, January 3, 1954, although too frothy to take seriously, does contain one astute observation: the collection succeeds best in those scenes where the parents have the least to say and the reader can observe Cress directly without intermediary interpretation. The book does seem one written for children in just those places, but only those places, where the elder Delahantys speak. Incidentally, none of the reviewers seemed to question that the book is properly one for children and adults alike. The cautious Eleanor Scott wrote in the *Saturday Review* (January 9, 1954), having seen perhaps too many treatments of adolecents already on the market, that "these stories are very true and very good without attaining the highest distinction either in style or in content." Yet it would be quite a task to ascertain just how *Cress Delahanty* does fall short, if it does, of the "highest distinction" in content and style; and Miss Scott omits to give the criteria. *Cress Delahanty* most certainly has much of the subtlety and depth and humor and wisdom associated with great art. The essence of growing up, its quickenings, its high-minded enthusiasms, its dewy loves, its tremors of apprehension—all are here. (Someone is sure to add, with justice, that it is a more beautiful childhood than most people have known.)

IV *Cactus and Yellow Violets*

Still more daringly sexual than *Witch Diggers*, but not markedly risqué as compared with many works of the present era, *South of the Angels* is the most ambitious of the West stories up to 1960.[19] For the imagined little old lady teetering on her front porch rocking chair on Main Street in Whittier, *South of the Angels* must nevertheless have seemed south of the angels indeed! It is Miss West's longest fictional work by over a hundred pages, contains over thirty characters, most of whom are thoroughly developed, and is complex enough to make the average reader wish that the author had furnished a dramatis personae. This novel will rank for future generations as being among her best two or three books.[20]

The time at the beginning of the story is 1916, and the locale is the Tract, as the new settlers call it, that is situated twenty-five miles southeast of Los Angeles and about half that distance from Whittier and the Olinda oil fields. Geographically, this would be Yorba Linda, a fact confirmed by Miss West in her letter to Mr. Mock (see earlier). Her childhood friend, Gladys Gauldin, who knows the region, affirms that " 'South of the Angels' . . . describes Yorba Linda [as it was in their girlhood] very well" and that many of the incidents are taken from Jessamyn's life. She then says that some Yorba Lindans "resented" portions of the book, feeling they could identify such and such characters from among the community.[21] In *South of the Angels* the physical community, then, closely resembles the Yorba Linda of history, but the people involved are generally fictitious, for as Miss West says in a letter to Mr. Mock, "God forbid that anyone find any resemblances between the characters in *that* book [*South of the Angels*] and anybody, Milhous or non-Milhous, living or dead!"

Nonetheless, there remains the curious, but only curious, parallel that in 1914, just three years before a similar incident in the novel, a group of Yorba Linda stockholders brought a successful lawsuit against Janss Investment Company because of its handling of the incorporated water company.[22] As this suit went as far as the United State Supreme Court, it does seem inevitable that a certain twelve-year-old girl in the township would hear about it—as stated earlier, the community was extremely small, and her own father was at one time the superintendent of the water company. What further correlations between the real and the fictional lawsuit exist are unknown to me.

The many ramifications of the story permit only a skeleton summary here. At least six separate families, some of them Quakers, plus a few bachelors move to the Tract where they live in tents until permanent dwellings can be erected. The agricultural problem of securing water is matched by the emotional problems of loneliness and sexual frustration and eagerness of the young to find sweethearts. Among these sufferers are the Copes, consisting of the newspaperman Lute; his wife Indiana Rose (called Indy), who was formerly separated from him but returns in time to have an affair with the carpenter Tom Mount; and two daughters, one of whom, Press, is the story's beautiful heroine who has reached the dangerous age of seventeen. Press is in love with a neighbor lad named Chad Lewis, but she withholds herself from him out of a guilty feeling that she owes her mother special attention. After she learns how faithless Indy has been, the filial bond is broken. Other love relationships, at least eight of them not counting the married ones, help tie together the dwellers of the Tract.

Several additional unifying features operate. First in order is the physical Tract itself in which everyone has a not-too-clear title to a piece of land and where they all share in a clamor for water rights. The lake which they meanwhile use in common furnishes opportunities for neighborly gossip. Next comes the "lucky" bed in the Lewis household upon which Pete and Rosa Ramos, and later Shel and Joicey Lewis, conceive their latest offspring.

Other unifying elements consist of the two main themes running through the novel, the first of which is the Love-Fertility-Death cycle, the love particulars of which have already been indicated. But something more should be said about the roué Tom Mount who, around unattached and lonely women, "was a real miser of persons. He liked to keep a good supply on hand, even though there were some he might never get around to using"(429). Although Tom's unions with Opal, Eunice, Indy, and Crystal are so much fruitless fornication, it is different with the other mating couples of the area. The birth of a calf at one farm foreshadows the human fertility. When the essential water has arrived to fertilize the crops, and exactly at the end of the normal gestation period of nine months, the first babies are born. Just as the children arrive, as part of the fertility pattern, the birth pains of the agrarian experiment subside and the crops and trees are at last growing.

Foreshadowing of death comes early in the story with the severe tubercular illness of Mrs. Waite, who is hardly expected to live. At the end of the novel, as if to offset the birth of the two children, there is the awesome coincidence of two deaths on that same night: Pete Ramos and the hopeless invalid Mary Jessup. And so death neatly balances out life, and the little world of the Tract goes on. As we can see, the novel is structurally interesting.

Possibly Miss West has an acquaintance with such seminal works on the fertility myth as Sir James Frazer's *The Golden Bough,* Jessie Weston's *From Ritual to Romance,* and almost certainly T. S. Eliot's derivative poem *The Waste Land.* In any case, the quarter of a century of farm life behind Miss West illustrated for her the great round of nature, of budding leaf, of flower, of fruit, of fallen or barren branch, and must have intimated to the symbol-conscious artist in her the concept of nature as metaphor for man's mortality. Of the almost limitless possibilities for this kind of influence, not to be dismissed is the author's own close brush with death and the record of family calamity—a surprising amount of serious illness and death by disease.[23]

In the second theme, that of ironic fulfillment, old Mary Jessup has spent almost a lifetime believing she never loved her husband because she could not forget a certain Chester Bannister who had once jilted her to run off with a widow. As Mary is dying from some undisclosed ailment, she at last comprehends, with Wendlin's help, that she has actually always loved him. The relief she gains from this realization enables her to die in peace, and she even forgets that she was contemplating suicide. Like Jess Birdwell and Mr. Cornelius, she gains from the prospect of death such a heightened awareness of the beauties and pleasures of ordinary living that she is positively radiant.

The companionship of Mary Jessup taught her friend, Asa Brice, that something crucial was missing in the solitary bachelordom of raising a garden and inspecting snowstorms and taking down nature notes; namely, human affection in the form of lover or wife. When he first arrived, he thought that his individualistic approach to living would bring him happiness; it never did. He felt the eternal need of any human soul, whether he dwelt by Walden Pond or California arroyo: "recently the wind, which he had espoused and which he knew to be ungrieving, grieved him. Overhead, the stars, his children, blazing in the winter sky, left his heart empty. He was ready to be delighted by any show of humanness . . ." (410). The poetry intensifies and takes on anguish when Asa answers the missionary Paula Jessup, home visiting her dying mother, who wanted to know what the stars spoke when he gazed on high:

"Nothing," Asa declared. "They say nothing to me except that they are distant and blazing and speechless. And not one fact that I can learn about them reconciles me for a minute to a harder fact, that we are alive beneath them and cannot communicate our loneliness. One world at a time, Miss Jessup, one world at a time. Until I can open my heart to one person here, what heart have I got to take into eternity with me? That stone in my chest? Add that stone to God's firmament of light? Your mother [Mary Jessup, now dead] was more to me than any star. . . ."

"You must reconcile yourself to God's plan, Mr. Brice," Paula said.

Asa jumped to his feet. "I am not reconciled to the leaden life we lead. I am not reconciled to loneliness. . . . You ask me about God's firmament . . . and the stars in it. That is eternity, if you like, and when I go into it, all I'm going to be able to say to the shining stars is, 'Stars, I have noticed that you shine.' That is my life. And it's not enough. It is no answer to pain and death. To balance them there must be something else." (510-11)

As every reader of the novel knows, this eloquent and attractive figure falls in love with one of Mount's former mistresses, Eunice Frye.

Asa, a kind of Thoreau, is ironically treated and humanized for the needs of a love plot; we might add that he is written about in *South of the Angels* from the *feminine* point of view, as if it were universally agreed that a bachelor in possession of his freedom must be in want of a wife. Asa is content to let the next world take care of itself (given the famous line, "One world at a time"); and he gives short shrift to any conventional Christian interpretation of the divine plan. We learn also that he is stiff and reserved, watches the weather diligently, keeps track of the season's first blooms, has a keen sense of smell, likes walks, observes woodchucks and ants with absorbed curiosity, keeps a notebook, prefers to rough it outdoors even after others have retreated to living in houses, and dislikes war as well as he does organized society. To complete the nearly thorough portrait of the author of *Walden*, he is short and blond and has the big Emerson nose that Concord villagers said Thoreau was growing for himself. No wonder Jessamyn West was scanning the journals of Thoreau in her Hollywood motel room in 1955, during the time the novel was underway![24]

Even so, Asa emerges in the story as a distinct personality, aside from his attributes of the great Transcendentalist; moreover, he utters some of the most puissant lines in all of Jessamyn West. The portrayal is unquestionably skillful as compared with what Stratton-Porter did with her Thoreau-figure in *The Harvester*; and it at least equals the handling of another such figure (Van Dorn) in Maxwell Anderson's drama *High Tor*. (Incidentally, Thoreau himself figures in Miss West's incomparably touching story "Like Visitants of Air.")

Indy is another character in *South of the Angels* who suffers loneliness, not for lacking a mate but for being married to the wrong one. Through adultery she has learned what it is like to be a sexually rejuvenated woman; but, by the time her carnal indiscretions have taught her what she has been missing at home, Lute learns of the affair; and, by appealing to her sense of pity for him, he tricks her into becoming his willing prisoner. Their confrontation in Book IV, Chapter 4, is a masterful study in human psychology.

Lute, having thus ensnared his wife again, still cannot win from her the love he wants. All that this emotional dwarf knows to do whenever Indy is lonely is to give her his simplistic "cure" of another bed session, a remedy that, even with her new ardency gained from Mount, leaves her at best dutifully passive. This passivity tantalizes and spurs him on to virtual rapes as he tries to make his victim say whether her experience is pleasure or pain. Sphinxlike, she denies him real gratification; and she unwittingly urges him on to new violations and to ever new remorse because of them. As a result, he longs for some cleansing that will end his torment. A psychologist would observe that he is afflicted with a sado-masochistic syndrome. Behind his mental sickness is his hatred for Tom Mount; he takes out this hatred on his wife in sexual aggression.

The roots of his problem are partly Freudian, extending back to childhood where Lute's mother found no pleasure in married sex, envisioned the wife's role as a stoic, and passed on to her son her own dreadful inhibitions. If one is to believe what Miss West says elsewhere in her writings, a wholesome sex education in Lute's early years might have worked wonders for him. He is one of the most vivid and believable characters yet created by Jessamyn West.

When Indy does not fulfill her daughter's ideal of what a mother should be, Press, feeling free of her, runs off and gives herself to Chad in a wild gamble to insure herself happiness. The reader is told that Chad would make an unforgivable mistake if he rejected her now; "if he suggested postponement, Press might understand with her mind. But her body wouldn't understand. Her body might never forgive him, and he couldn't risk that. She his wife, but her body, for the rest of their lives, his enemy" (459). As Press's own father had in his day repelled Indy in such circumstances just before they were married, we cannot doubt within the logic of the novel the emotional alienation this rejection might have caused, despite any moral considerations that might be presented. What is ironic about Press's act is the fact that the hitherto restrained girl finally throws herself at the suitor who had long but vainly solicited her love.

Miss West assumes, of course, that the woman's emotional organization is so much more sensitive than the man's that the woman alone is liable to suffer an erotic trauma under the circumstances depicted above. If her assumption is correct, it opposes the male tradition that believes the woman is naturally capable of and is obligated to have the greater self-control over the temptations of sex. In *Love Is Not What You Think,* which among other things is an impassioned essay on the spiritual qualities associated with physical love, Miss West furnishes a gloss on the problem at hand.[25] Among various authorities on love, she cites Albert Camus several times approvingly in her rationale for a romantic, intuitive approach. She could have had Press Cope on her mind when she wrote the following, for the essay and the novel were published only a year apart: "All love is a meeting. It is sorrowful for a woman if she is not met in all the potentialities of her nature; sorrowful for anyone, *but most sorrowful for a woman* [italics mine], who needs to be encompassed by her lover. Still, a woman had better, if faced by that bitter predicament, go against her judgment than against her senses. A woman judges with her senses. There is no use telling her that something which she does not feel to be right is right" (23). This is, then, not only the guide that Press follows but what Cate Conboy in *Witch Diggers* failed to follow—to her misery. There is the consolation that young Press will at least be able to avoid one of the greatest mistakes of her parents, for her heart offering is not turned down.

Not so with Crystal Raunce, who in the Tract's newspaper office one day confesses to Lute her innocent love for him. Shocked, he rudely rejects her; for the Puritan in him is unable to disassociate love from sex, and he bluntly tells her to suppress her imagination. Plain-featured little Crystal, who means well but is unable to win any boys or men through openly declared affection, turns away brokenheartedly from Lute, who should have helped her with understanding and kindness; and she soon consorts with the philanderer Tom Mount in her quest for affection. The innocent fulfillment she wants is impossible in the kind of love he has to offer.

The theme of ironic fulfillment surfaces elsewhere as well. Crystal's vulgar father, LeRoy Raunce, whose theology told him that he was "saved" and therefore "sinless," had built a church with the expectation that he would naturally be chosen its minister; unfortunately, a false accusation of indecency destroys his chances for the post. Pete Ramos believed that having a son would represent for him the fullness of manhood; consequently, it is a bitter irony that on the night of his son's birth he should be slain defending the life of a friend who was trying to *evade* the responsibilities of paternity.

The case of Sylvester Perkins, developer of the Tract, represents the fall of an idealist, a man appropriately represented by the mountain tops toward which he habitually gazes from his office window. His aim from the beginning had been altruistic in wanting every one of the settlers to lead a good life in a beautiful place: "He never saw a kid out in the Tract chasing a tumbleweed, or a housewife watering a geranium, but his heart melted with pleasure" (436). When he had settled his clients on the land, they then show their gratitude by suing him because he had secretly mortgaged the Water Company in order to raise the money needed for irrigation pipes. In short, Perkins was unlucky. Louella, his wife, undergoes an unexpected fulfillment, too. From the beginning, she had thought her scheming husband a fraud; and she had resolved that she would leave him someday whenever someone else would prove to her his guilt. When he loses his court trial, she surprises herself by not reacting at all as expected. Her discovery of how she truly feels about this rare man parallels to some extent the case of Mrs. Jessup and her husband.

South of the Angels exemplifies some ways in which Miss West treats her male figures. Open physical conflict is, as usual, underplayed; and the little there is of it is reported by a third party. The practice of having some of her men kneel before their women may strike the reader as old-fashioned. Perkins thinks of dropping to his knees before Louella when she is ready to comfort him. Pete falls to his knees before Rosa after their child has arrived. And Lute kneels before Indy and covers his face with her skirts, squinting out slyly at times to see what effect his pleading might have.

Moreover, Miss West's males are not especially *aggressive* as lovers, and they are rarely linguistically offensive when speaking of sex; they appear to represent the average in maleness. Christie Fraser, as seen in an earlier novel, is a fair example of the type. Mount is, of course, at the other end of the libidinal spectrum, a rake and without scruples; and, besides, he is rather lazy and passive as a lover, although he is vain enough about his bodily powers. His fornication scene in Fort Collins is oddly lacking in virility; he seems almost tired, like a sluggish python in a tree waiting for his game to pass beneath. So seemingly indifferent is this otherwise erotic animal that on an occasion, when he sees Indy bathing nude in her yard, he, like a gentleman, turns his head the other way. The peruser of the hairy-chested novels of James Jones would find Mount comparatively effeminate.

In the West books the truly aggressive people, the pursuers, the sexy-talking ones, are the women. When it comes to sheer forwardness, Mount, for all his conquests—insofar as they are shown in the novel—cannot hold a candle to Press and Medora. Much less can shy Ortiz, who has to be hunted down before he will consent to wrong Medora. As for dirty expressions and vile four-lettered words, Opal and this same Medora have all but cornered the market in *South of the Angels.* We do not intend to say that the men are not believably coarse or masculine enough to sustain the demands today for some measure of Realism. Unquestionably, some readers are going to be offended with what coarseness the men do have. But Jessamyn West is relatively delicate-minded as compared with many of her contemporary authors, but still she is much franker than Henry James or Edith Wharton ever tried to be.

The critical reception of *South of the Angels* left more than a little to be desired. William Hogan, an avowed champion of the novelist, complimented her in the *Saturday Review* (April 23, 1960) on her craftsmanship, yet urged, unconvincingly, that she ought not to have chosen a big canvas—the "pageant" being too long and overpopulated. Hogan seemed to miss completely the cleverly arranged contrasts and parallels (ruin of the orange trees, and, simultaneously, Mary's dying), the ironies, the ingenious *double-entendres*, the surprising verbal linkups between chapters and scenes (see Book I, Chapters 2-3), and the thoroughness, let alone the complexity, of the numerous characterizations. Orville Prescott in the *San Francisco Chronicle* (April 28, 1960) omitted to mention any unified pattern or patterns; still, he fretted that the book is too concerned with sexual passion. The *Atlantic* (July, 1960) carried Edward Weeks's brief but suave and appreciative views, including one that the story contains "many gleaming moments . . ." (96). The most unqualified praise of all came from R. T. Bresler in the *Library Journal* (May 15, 1960), who hailed it as a "beautifully written book." And it is.

To summarize, none of the reviewers recorded any significant structural unity; and several thought the work too long and the characters too many. As shown earlier, *South of the Angels* is well unified by several different methods. In the eyes of almost any scholar or serious critic, the objection of excessive length in a novel, or of too many characters, is tantamount to frivolousness unless the objection is accompanied by valid reasons (nowhere to be seen in the reviews). Possibly, the assumption that repeatedly leads some reviewers astray in the case of Jessamyn West's later books is that, since she has written some so-called simple, honest, and straightforward stories about Quakers and adolescents, she is not going to be complicated or clever in anything different. Hence, her powers are frequently underestimated.

In *South of the Angels* there is much to admire. There is the naturalness of it all, with the story ending as an episode in life might; for a certain inconclusiveness still prevails in spite of all the answers that are supplied. The story ends as it should—in accord with the logical demands of character and situation. The life-cycle theme insures that no neat ending is feasible.

V *Sister, Dear Sister*[26]

The controversial novel *A Matter of Time*, serialized in *Redbook* in 1966 and issued in the fall in hard covers, has not drawn popular acclaim. But the work shows that the author's vitality and clearsightedness were still intact, even if tempered by a deepening sense of mortality. The writing of *A Matter of Time* took two years, during which period Jessamyn West placed a group of indifferent short stories in *Good Housekeeping, Harper's*, and *Ladies' Home Journal*. It could be that she was reserving her skill for the momentous "breakthrough into present time and reality," as she later referred to the novel, whose story was so sensational and so agonizing to write as to make her truly believe that it would never be published.

"[P]erhaps only this belief [that it might not be published] permitted me to write it," she adds.[27]

The story proceeds on two levels; first, it follows events in the present time in which Blix, dying in her desert home, enlists the aid of her older librarian-sister, Tasmania (called Tassie), and her physician, Dr. Reyes, to poison herself when her cancer becomes hopelessly enlarged and excruciating. Beautiful Blix, consciously named by her mother after Frank Norris' heroine, is now middle-aged; and, like Tassie, she is in her second marriage, for their first marriages had been failures. Blix's latest husband is an auto dealer who visits there occasionally, at which time he demonstrates grief in the manner now fashionable in novels and motion pictures by drinking whiskey. He is a nonentity.

The second and, by far, the more interesting level consists of the flashbacks that Tassie has of remembered experiences as she converses with her dying sister. Consequently, they come to understand the whys and wherefores of much they have gone through and they clear up misunderstandings. In fact, much of the story might be called "The Education of Tassie." In the flashbacks, and even flashbacks within flashbacks, to the days of their childhood, courtship, and early marriage, we learn that Tassie was from the beginning eager to please her mother, the sickly Maude Murphy. And the mother is needlessly and puritanically suspicious about Blix's sex life.

As sisters, Blix and Tassie are sharply differentiated. Blix, the family beauty, is hard to please; is a rebel; is generous to a fault; is a good dresser; and is knowledgeable about where to eat and places to go; moreover, she attracts too many males for her mother's peace of mind. Meanwhile, plain Tassie, unlucky in luring men, takes pride in withdrawing and in conforming, in being self-righteous and pure; and she always remains above suspicion—it follows that she is also spared real adventure. She continually shrinks from committing herself to either optimism or joy. As a stoic, she stands for a phase which the author herself once passed through, therefore suggesting that Tassie is an alter ego acting out in imaginary ways the unfortunate withdrawal which helped keep the author so long from the literary scene.

The failure of parents, church, and college to prepare Tassie for congenial mating makes it possible for her to go to the altar with a selfish prig named Everett.[28] Like Cate Conboy, Tassie makes a point of ignoring the ample warnings of friends by marrying Everett; indeed, the impression generated is that, if she would only obey the all-important choice of her body, of her senses rather than of her mind, in accordance with the philosophy in *Love Is Not What You Think*, she would quickly have dropped this cold young man. Webster Schott points out in his perceptive review in *Life* that her first marriage is "the logical outcome of a Christian neurosis that said give but do not take."[29]

In addition to Everett's other defects, he is an all-around failure at making a living. Meanwhile, lonely Tassie forms a habit of falling in love with various men such as Manuel, the Mexican apricot picker, and never does anything about it. To her mind, the secret desire is everything; the fulfillment, unnecessary.

Blix, *too* receptive to boys, and better informed about sex than her sister, has an affair with a handsome priapic wonder named Vurl. When the mother discovers abortion equipment in Blix's purses, she persuades Tassie to break up the union by dishonest means. Tassie readily cooperates and once more shows herself to be "mama's girl." One thing Tassie learns from her sickroom conversations is that her having ended the affair had produced an unexpected change: Blix's values altered from loose giving to calculated taking so that, when she did leave off incontinence to get married, it was solely for material considerations—no more of letting the heart rule the head.

In the reminiscences other members of the Murphy family are introduced, including the father, Orland, who was always too absorbed at tinkering with the radio to concern himself with the children's sex problems; Blackie, the imaginative little redheaded brother; Marmion, another brother, a dead weight as a personality, who had early set himself against anything so immature as enthusiasm; and lastly, Le Cid, another of the oddly named children, who is openly scornful of Christian orthodoxy and who alone of the offspring has the independence to break away finally from the stultifying community and church to lead an enviable life among London theatrical folk. "I was less at ease with Le Cid than with any of the others," Tassie admits about this apostate from the Pilgrim Church. "Le Cid's number I didn't have" (51). This admission is not surprising, for his is no timid, milksop constitution like hers; he represents the defiant individualism that causes young people to decide to be themselves and to live their own lives. But Le Cid's flaw, and it is a big one, is that he has relinquished his religious heritage and has found no other religion to replace it.

One of the charming things about the story is the close-knit, fun-loving, and exciting family circle, in spite of the relative poverty of their recreational resources. Yet, when it comes to religion, the Murphys are content to ignore or be ignorant of primary religious experience. Their church attendance is perfunctory. Since their removal from Kentucky, where membership in the sect carried responsibilities, all but Tassie lack any yearning to *do* something as a sign of spiritual conviction. They never observe religious holidays or consider giving charity to the poor. The parents sometimes read the Bible aloud, but they grow silent when the children approach. *A Matter of Time* delineates through such passages the desuetude and worldliness that have befallen Protestant religions, particularly Quakerism, on the West Coast, now that the early pioneer stage has passed and with it the old strengths and certainties.

The father in the family is vaguely drawn and basically uninteresting. On the other hand, Maude, with her bloomer-girl prudishness, does come to life as a joint wrongdoer with her husband and as a personality who, aside from her faults, richly stimulated Tassie's imagination. In reading Tassie's tribute to her mother, we inevitably see behind the winsome anecdotist the shade of Grace West, altered in some way, maybe, but still there: "Listening to Mother, I learned to live where I wasn't. Compelled by her art, I had my most vivid life in her memories. I imagined those hills and branches, those creeks and springs; the Aunt Libs and Uncle Steves, the Great-grandfather Amoses and Grandmother Elizas. And everything we imagine is, because it is a part of ourselves, more real than reality. It is the reality *we* have manufactured. We possess it, as God does the world *He* created. It is the dust into which we have blown the breath of life" (75-76). Later on, there is another poetic tribute to this woman, with much the same biographical overtones, this time a requiem on the subject of dust (186). The existence of these two printed passages illustrates, also, a quality that is endearing in Jessamyn West: a profound gratitude to those who have somehow enriched her life.

Next to Everett and Le Cid, Dr. Reyes is the best developed adult male characterization in the novel. For reasons sufficiently obvious by now, the author has had no little traffic with the medical profession; accordingly, her physicians always stand out in bold relief. Indeed, in deftness of portraiture they rival even the major characters in some stories.

In the climax of the novel, Blix, after learning from her doctor that her case is beyond all question hopeless, attires herself in a green silk dress, symbolic of the abundant living to which she is bidding farewell and of the green earth she will soon join, she anoints her body with perfume, applies silver nail polish, and as the final part of her ritual takes a handful of capsules from a gilt-edged toothpick holder. She dies bravely and makes of her final act what the author prefers to call a "celebration of life." Miss West means by this last phrase that Blix demonstrates her control over her own life, refuses to be a victim, and manages to keep to the end as much of her humanity as possible.[30] One valid objection readers might make is that Pete and Milt, the husbands of these women, accede to suicide with just a bit too much readiness to be typical spouses; one or the other of them surely ought to have held out long enough to provoke some revealing arguments pro and con.

A Matter of Time is a collective tragedy with respect to the theme of religious privation among the Murphy family and the theme of marital misfortune among the daughters. Another tragedy involves the theme of euthanasia. Blix is defeated on her own terms; she is courageous in the teeth of despair. But the tragic impact of Blix's conquest over pain is lessened in two ways. First, the tragic role is relegated to a secondary figure. Hardly anyone who reads the book can deny that the primary interest inheres in Tassie, a character decidedly less courageous than her sister. Second, the American reading public is not yet Roman enough to accept with either welcome or complacency the prospect of suicide, no matter how distressed the victim; or, in this instance, to admire anyone for presuming to go through with what is considered a sin by many Christians and a sign of abnormalcy by most Occidentals.[31] No one can deny, however, that the two essentials of tragedy in all ages, courage and inevitable defeat, are clearly marked in the brief career of Blix Murphy. One of the problems in taking the novel seriously is the conflict between the favorable treatment given suicidal euthanasia (definitely unsettling with the Christian conscience) and the lament Tassie voices about the lack of Christian conviction and practice.

As Felicia Lamport correctly noted in her review in *Book Week* (November 6, 1966), the imagery is often vivid, sometimes strikingly so. Miss West proves herself once again adept at sensuous nature description, as where, for example, she describes a hot summer afternoon in California: "The valley smelled like a country kitchen, wood range fired up and jam kettle bubbling. Cherries, apricots, peaches, plums; all had come to a rolling boil. The ripening vegetables had a bland, starchy smell, a man smell, as contrasted with the female smell of the acid-sweet fruits" (164). Characteristically, her description of nature is at the level of leaf and bud and fruit, with their attendant sensuousness and even domestic associations; she does not present a whole sweep of landscape after the manner of, say, James Fenimore Cooper. The passage about the dragonfly in Book XII is a resplendent example of her method, and it fittingly emblematizes Blix's translation to a better world after death—if suicides are admitted to that place. In a marsh some larvae worms sadly discuss what has befallen one of their lost neighbors and misunderstand the glorious transformation that has taken place; meanwhile, the mourned one, rid of his chrysalis shell, has soared off into an undreamed-of light. The inspiration might possibly have been found in Alfred Lord Tennyson's "The Two Voices," where he has the suicidal voice cite the newly transformed dragonfly as an example of freedom through death.

The most obvious difference between this work and her earlier works is that she voices for the first time a definitely controversial issue of contemporary importance. The novel is also different in that it is narrated in the first person and has some of the story occur in the present time. There is, in addition, a more frequent and, at times, a more sustained handling of poetic and rhetorical technique than usual. Examples of the former have already been given. The sentences are often as finely etched and as stalwart as a Damascene blade. A certain nervous energy cuts through the prose, urgent, passionate (partly owing to the passionate nature of Blix herself), as if we were in the presence of a long-delayed confession that will not be put off any longer. The writing is a change for Jessamyn West in other ways, too. Epigrams make their appearance, such as "Cowards may die many deaths, but the doomed experience many resurrections" (206); "A hospital by definition is a place where when they make tea, water results" (183). Maude's biblical rhythms in her letter to Tassie itemizing the cares of hospital life are diluted by the sadness that suffuses much of the book.

Elaine Gottlieb in the *New York Times Book Review* (October 16, 1966) mentions a certain "lack of depth" in the depiction of secondary characters. For this reviewer, the portraits of Blix and Tassie were compelling enough to make the others, however, seem unimportant. In defense of Miss West, we could add that some of the minor characters, such as Maud, Vurl, and the lesbian nurse, are memorably if slightly sketched. Most of the reviews, including Miss Gottlieb's, were mainly complimentary. This applies to the one by Charles Poore, too, found in the daily edition of the *New York Times* (October 27, 1966). Poore nevertheless objected to the "awkward" naming of the characters, as if Miss West were not justified in this practice. As a matter of record, she has her Tassie bring up this very peculiarity.

We should note, nonetheless, that Jessamyn West selects her names patiently with due regard for wanted connotations. Marmion, for example, seems to be a pun on *mar*; he likes to mar any joyous impulse that might perchance spring up in his breast. Le Cid connotes an adventurous, romantic figure, which is rather what he turns out to be finally. Tassie reminds us of *tassel*, a slight device without much inner strength and which depends from some support, a meaning applicable to the girl's emotional dependence, first upon her mother and later upon her sister. Vurl, the aggressive and athletic seducer, would dearly like to *curl* up with a *girl*, even Tassie, as one passionate scene reveals. The word also suggests *cur*. It has an unpleasant combination of consonants—as Tassie duly notes; for the animal growl of the *r* lurks between a soft, fricative *v* and the purling liquid of an *l*. The sound is both voluptuous and repellent. And, as a final touch of eroticism, overdone in this instance, his surname is none other than Seaman. The names of Blix and Blackie convey ironic implications: Norris' Blix comes to a happy ending in his book; Blackie has red hair. The name Murphy could have been chosen for its very commonness, in addition to being Irish—a favored race in West books.

The Hollywood scriptwriting experience had an indirect influence on the construction of *A Matter of Time*. So stimulating was the experience of being questioned on her methods by studio officials that she solicited similar challenging inquiries from her editor at Harcourt, Brace and World; and these were readily supplied. The ultimate value of this intensified editorial comment is difficult to assess, however, beyond the point of cautious speculation. After the manuscript of *A Matter of Time* had already undergone an enormous amount of cutting before it left Napa for the first time, Julian Muller advised an additional cut of about a hundred pages.[32]

By now it is clear that *A Matter of Time* has yet to catch on with the public to the degree enjoyed by *Friendly Persuasion* and *Cress Delahanty*—invitingly "pleasant" books—despite its sensational subject matter and technical excellence. The unpleasant subject of suicide does not, of course, doom a book to obscurity, as several modern classics can well attest. But in addition to permitting the suicide-religion conflict, the author may have erred in being too sympathetic with the family whose faults she depicts. Some of the Murphys are made so attractive that we forget, at times, the implied criticism of the family's moral and religious life. If the author's spokesman, Tassie, who comments sometimes upon the Murphy weaknesses, had not been so fond of that family as to find in its reunions one of her chief sources of pleasure, the shortcomings might have been more manifest. But this objection is a minor one. Loving and finding fault are not impossible companions.

One problem external to the novel is that the ordinary reader of today is part of a religiously lax era and has few if any misgivings about being so; the Murphy habits of irregular church attendance (two or three times monthly) and indifferent formalism are not much unlike his own. Such habits therefore seem innocently normal. Moreover, such a person meets in the book no such aids as comic satire or models of behavior to alert and guide him in interpretation. As a casual reader, he does not readily see the Quaker sect disguised under the label "Puritan." And he may altogether fail to perceive that the author is judging the trends of modern Quakerism by reference to some standards not made explicit in the text, standards of an earlier age such as the Birdwells knew. Consequently, the novel may give the impression of excessive understatement, of a withholding of evidence for the indictment. Anyone who intends to read *A Matter of Time* would do well to read *Friendly Persuasion* first, so that he can see how far the Murphys have strayed from the simple, beautiful, wholesome ways of Quaker family life and worship.

The novel signals a new direction for Jessamyn West, one which she is well pleased to take at long last: the contemporary scene. Whether *A Matter of Time* marks any improvement in her art, or is merely a pause before some greater venture, may be of little consequence inasmuch as she has already wrought enough to make her be remembered wherever good books are enjoyed.

Insofar as the origin of *A Matter of Time* can be pieced together from details available, Miss West's story "Reverdy" furnished some matter, the younger sister there assuming the role of the older, and vice versa. Suggestive but not directly contributory is "Another Word Entirely," a work printed in the *New Mexico Quarterly* in the spring of 1947, about a pair of girls, one of whom has an abortion following an adulterous romance.

The memory of various relatives in the family who were killed by cancer, including her sister Carmen, plus the thought that she herself might be afflicted someday, inspired Miss West to explore in fiction what she thought she might do in a similar situation where the agony was increasing and nearly unrelievable.[33] In *A Matter of Time* there are any number of veiled connections with the author's familial background, but these have undergone change to form patterns rich and strange. Linda in the present story, for example, reflects Yorba Linda. The apricot orchard evokes memories of Hemet; Pilgrim College, a small, humdrum church school twenty-five miles from Los Angeles, is the counterpart of Whittier College;[34] Tassie's serious illness parallels Miss West's tuberculosis. Inescapably, the Pilgrim Church intimates West Coast Quakerism, although it could as easily refer to some long-established Puritan sects in America. In the Whittier district during the author's girlhood, there was little to distinguish the Methodists and the Baptists from the Quakers, save for communion and baptism; for they all sang in church (Jess Birdwell, for example, was born too soon!), heard preaching, and attended revivals. In a letter to me, dated December 20, 1966, Miss West clinches the identification when she says that " 'A Matter of Time' was The Friendly Persuasion family *now*; the emptiness of much Quakerism *now*" (italics hers).

Felt throughout the book is the intimate and affectionate regard known to exist between Jessamyn West and her parental family;[35] but, let it be remembered, the fictional Murphy family is exposed for its irresponsibility and error and spiritual privation. The portrait of Mrs. Murphy owes much to the ailing Grace West of her later years; Blackie suggests the young Merle; and, in my well-considered judgment, Blix's soft beauty is borrowed from Carmen who, as an early photograph shows, was physically attractive in no small degree.

VI *An Autumn Gathering*

September of 1970 brought the windfall of *Crimson Ramblers of*

the World, Farewell.[36] One special advantage of this new harvest
was to let the reader taste some of the very earliest flavors, like
"99.6" and "The Day of the Hawk," hitherto accessible only in back
issues of obscure periodicals. The collection is quite diverse in subject matter and in quality, all of which is understandable because of
the long span of time represented by some of the writings. Many
selections do, however, share in common a young female narrator or
heroine, who is identified differently in each case, and who is troubled by or witness to some affair of the heart. As explained much
earlier, the two stories just cited echo Miss West's own tubercular
crisis in the sanatorium; another such story, maybe the best of the
trio, is a study in female cruelty named "I'll Ask Him to Come
Sooner." In the last, a not-so-ladylike patient waylays the husband
of her fellow inmate with the intention, she piously tells herself,
of upbraiding him for always being late to visit his distressed wife;
instead, she ends up in his embraces because all along she had
merely desired him for herself.

The title story, a new one, proves that this durable Quakeress has
not lost her knack at capturing those crucial, formative moments in
the young when the soul is shaped for good or for ill. In the story,
Mrs. Prescott catches her adolescent daughter Elizabeth at the knot-
hole one morning as she accidentally stares down at her father
who is bathing nude in the kitchen, scolds her that this "spying" is
evil and perverted, and tells her that she has tendencies to be
guarded against most rigidly. Guilt-stricken because she feels that
her mother must be right, the impressionable innocent plays traitor
to her natural feelings the next day at school and rejects the love
overtures of her new and promising boyfriend, the colorful Crimson Rambler. Hers is a mother fixation aborning, prelude to what
Sidney Howard handled in his drama on the dangers of mother love,
The Silver Cord. The story is exceptional.

"Night Piece for Julia"—the title echoes Herrick but also smacks
of a *double-entendre*—portrays another examination of sex fear,
one that points out what Elizabeth's repression might logically lead
to in adult years: the heroine Julia steels herself against pain before
she submits to bedtime joys with her husband. Perhaps it will not
be supererogatory to assert that in West books this popular Freudianism, the crippling power of sex fear and repression, is a common
feature.

Still one more excursion into sex is "Mother's Day," which gains its punch from a double-surprise ending. Merlin goes with her husband, Alban, already shown as petted and pleased with wifely attentions, to check on reports that Aunt El-Dora is having to share her husband with another woman for five days out of seven and does not relish the arrangement. It comes as a jolt when they see El-Dora and her weekend wooer together in conjugal harmony, cooing and billing as if they were newlyweds or lovers. Moreover, to Merlin's alarm, her Alban believes that the split ménage arrangement must be simply wonderful, for the husband enjoys not merely the loving attentions of his wife but at other times the company of his talented mistress. Miss West's candid approach is what especially pleases here. She sets forth the wish-fulfillment of the universal married male who surrendered his heart before he had quite understood how deeply polygamous he was and dared to follow that instinct into practice.

In "Live Life Deeply" Jessamyn West fictionalizes the near-tragic conflict with the neurotic college English teacher mentioned in *To See the Dream.* "Child of the Century" chronicles the sad but somehow grimly comic misadventures of one Oliver Young, whose birth at precisely the turn of 1900 is interpreted by his ambitious mother as auguring conspicuous success for him. The story hinges on the problem of too much influence from the parent—a common theme in West books. Finally a pharmacist, Oliver has gotten about as far in life as the farmer in the old joke, who was praised for his success, namely for being outstanding in his field.

The long-out-of-print item "Like Visitant of Air" is a thrilling discovery for many West devotees. The plot cleverly ties in two fiercely independent bachelors and nature lovers, Henry D. Thoreau and Emily Brontë, during the winter of 1845 when Thoreau lived alone and *lonely,* according to the author's feminist sympathies, in his rain-shrouded hut at Walden. Charlotte Brontë of the stormy English moors has just found Emily's poems which speak of her passionate yearnings for some lover and soul companion as yet unmet. Practically at the very moment when Emily affirms the reality of that companion somewhere, but knows in her despairing heart that she will never meet him in this world, Thoreau in a poignantly clairvoyant scene stands in the doorway of his hut and reaches out into the darkness and asks urgently, "Where are you? . . . Where are you?"

"The Heavy Stone" is not the sort of thing that comes natural to

Miss West—"it was outside me in spirit," she reports—and derives from a factual account told to her by a friend, who had lost a son in battle just recently on Luzon.[37] The story has the slickness and sentiment that popular ladies' magazines look for, although it was not written with that market in mind.[38] The still shorter "Gallup Poll," originally published also in *American Magazine*, is more sophisticated and thought-engaging. In a cocktail lounge, a woman in her thirties abruptly asks the other patrons to guess her age, the result to decide whether she will accept the proposal of nuptials made by her very young escort. Meanwhile, the upholstered "coffin lid" ceiling of the room, patently symbolic, hovers over the participants in this little drama and intensifies, at least for the reader, the value of youth and young love.

Canadian back country furnishes the locale in the comic "Hunting for Hootowls," whose boy-versus-adult relationships breathe forth some of the bouquet of childhood expected in vintage West. To Miss West, the unfamiliar Canadian landscape offers no problem: her husband, H. M. McPherson, has hunted wild game up there and doubtless could have supplied her with what little local color was needed.

As the horror-mystery story "Up a Tree" begins, a husband whose wife would not divorce him has already murdered her and hauled her body up to a platform in the trees where it could be devoured by buzzards; then, his daughter Eugenia, who disliked her mother but loved him inordinately, has discovered the crime and taken elaborate steps to conceal it.[39] Eugenia, from whose point of view the narration now unfolds in the present, sees to it that the police notice the right evidence, such as the fabricated farewell note and the sleeping pills, so that the death will seem a suicide and the father will get released from jail. Owing to the fragmentariness of her stream-of-consciousness revelations, we learn only indirectly of her complicity. Only as we notice her slips of tongue, her being the first to find the notebook and the pills, and her cold-blooded calm as she goes to sleep up there beside her mother's mortal remains, do we realize that here is another of those West figures who have been twisted out of normalcy by parental conflicts and displaced loyalties. It is the perfect crime, thanks to the daughter's foolishness. And the killer is scot-free to kill again. This is easily Jessamyn West's most chilling horror story to date, although the over-all excellence does not match that of "Dr. Chooney, M.D."

In the Land Where Lemons Bloom

There are at least two titles that should have been retrieved for the collection but were not: "The Ouija Board"[40] and "The Blackboard."[41] But by rounding up just about every uncollected West story of value, the editor performed a rich service. In many respects, particularly because of the widely unequal merit of some stories, the presence of the female narrator or heroine, the problem of love and marriage, the overinfluence from the parent, and the beguiling adolescent, the stories of *Crimson Ramblers* are on a par with those in *Love Death*. The tuberculosis theme in the early stories is markedly pronounced, reminder of a phase which Miss West has by now mostly abandoned in her craft. Disappointed love and unhappy marriage are still more prominent themes, figuring in over a third of the stories, specifically "Up a Tree," "There Ought to Be a Judge," "Crimson Ramblers," "Night Piece for Julia," "Like Visitant of Air," and "Child of the Century," a record illustrating that Jessamyn West was and still is absorbed—there is no better word for it—in domestic affairs of the heart as they are related to youth and marriage.

CHAPTER 4

Learn to Say Good-bye

I *Escape from the Genteel Tradition*

W HEN in 1925 the Englishwoman Maude Robinson issued her collection of pious and sentimental chronicles called *Wedded in Prison*,[1] the preface bore a revealing statement of the aims and limitations which a Quaker story writer might be expected to follow in using her talents to advance the church: "Nothing sensational will be found in these stories—no 'plots,' no 'villains of the piece,' but sketches from real life of men and women who lived and labored for the spreading of the Truth . . . and for the help and healing of their fellowmen." However improving such graceful sketches may be, they are sadly deficient in dramatic content; and the dialogue is wooden and monotonous. When compared with the sophisticated offerings of Jessamyn West, the Robinson stories are like superior exercises from a religious seminary. Yet these, too, enjoyed in their day a sizable acclaim, at least within the sect. Miss Robinson published this third collection mainly (she said) at the urging of her readers—a statement that is difficult for a non-Quaker to accept today, but it must be true, for most Quaker fictionists have not been able to surpass this English lady in craftsmanship.

That Jessamyn West has somehow escaped from the backwaters of the Genteel tradition represented by Miss Robinson and countless contemporary writers in and outside the Quaker faith is nothing less than astonishing if we pause to consider that the strength of the Genteel tradition in older members of the sect today is still a very real thing. We are tempted to add that, by remaining within the Society of Friends, Miss West must have felt a divided loyalty when she decided between or reconciled religious tradition and literary fashion. For instance, she somehow resisted the moralizing impulse in favor of the ostensibly amoral demands of objective art. Nor did she violate her innately gentle and humane disposition while she pursued the rigorous discipline of artistic "truth." As the most popular and the most gifted story writer the American Friends have yet had, she undoubtedly avoided along the way many an otherwise crippling inhibition. Open to question is whether her confessed stoicism detracted from the virility of her male characterizations.

II *Significance in Literature*

It would not be useful to compare Jessamyn West with such Hoosier writers as Edward Eggleston, Booth Tarkington, James W. Riley, Lew Wallace, Theodore Dreiser, and Ross Lockridge, although she contrasts interestingly with the obscure James Baldwin. Among the Hoosiers, the greatest similarity of all is with Gene Stratton-Porter, author of such once extremely popular sentimental novels as *Freckles* (1904) and *A Girl of the Limberlost* (1909). Both authors show a definite back-country Indiana locale, sympathetically render teen-aged heroes and heroines, possess a knowledgeable interest in natural history, and, indeed, each sketches at least one Thoreau figure in their respective books. Both women prepared some of their work for Hollywood filming.

As for differences, Jessamyn West's style is considerably more polished and objective than Stratton-Porter's was; and her work is not merely popular but definitely appeals to the intelligentsia. Furthermore, unlike Stratton-Porter, she, along with other twentieth-century writers, makes no claim that fiction should be morally improving, even though some portions of her *Friendly Persuasion*, *Except for Me and Thee*, and *Cress Delahanty* exude a subtle moral atmosphere. As Miss West is partly a California author, still another set of literary comparisons blossoms forth, though this influence is hardly so fruitful as the first. She is sufficiently original to deserve serious attention for her universal qualities and not simply for her regionalism or local-color tendencies.

Jessamyn West's contribution to national and world literature is her unique concern in her art about Quaker life in such works as *Friendly Persuasion* and *Except for Me and Thee*. Surely they have not been approached with such quality by any other writer anywhere. No one else in recorded literature has ever treated of the Quakers—definitely not the American branch of the sect—so extensively, so humanly, so entertainingly, and yet so faithfully to the spirit of historic truth even though the stories at hand are idealized in some particulars. That being as it may, those *cognoscenti* who treasure such techniques as wry understatement, symbolism, and psychological depth more than happy choice of subject matter,

sympathetic tone, and what can best be labeled with that old-fashioned word *inspiration*, might very well rank productions like *Love
Death* and *Crimson Ramblers* higher than the two Birdwell books.
For, in some ways, the Birdwell stories *are* simpler in texture, although this cannot be said of all of them; nevertheless, the main
characters in them are not "flat" ones in the sense of illustrating
one or two dominant traits at the expense of depth. They do come
alive—very much so. And that is what really matters after all.
Luckily, we do not have to choose between the two sets of works;
but, if we must, our taste would turn reluctantly in favor of the
Friendly Persuasion people, the ones we know best; not because we
dare not face up to evil, or think deeply, or contemplate the am-
biguities of human experience—we do all these things anyway in
the Birdwell books—but because there dwells in each of us a perennial desire for a Romantic interpretation of life, a desire left unsat-
isfied these days by the many specimens of raw and blatant Naturalism that clamor for our attention on the market, each of them
hawking its own peculiar brand of artistic "truth" or "reality."

Miss West's second distinction—although it is not a unique one—
is her literature about adolescence. Of course, books about adolescents have long been plentiful, and there are many good ones;
nevertheless, Miss West's *Friendly Persuasion, Cress Delahanty,
Love Death, South of the Angels*, and *Crimson Ramblers* stand out
in this class in a twofold way: (1) The high merit with respect to
sensitivity of characterizations, restraint, genuineness of feeling, psychology, and delightful humor. *Witch Diggers* belongs here too
except for some absence of restraint, but some of the most celebrated of recent authors—Thomas Wolfe, William Faulkner, and
Ernest Hemingway—seemed at times not to know what restraint
was! (2) The appeal of the first two books listed is not only to adults
but to children, and only a genuine storyteller reaches both groups.

In one of Sir James M. Barrie's early books, he observes that
genius is the capacity to prolong one's childhood. Whether measured against any other criterion or not, Jessamyn West beyond all
dispute qualifies here for her numerous figures of nonidealized
children. Nor does she subordinate the intrinsic interest in these to
the purpose of moral contrast with adults, unlike the purpose of J. D.
Salinger and William Golding. In Miss West's detailed sketches of
pert, intelligent, and nearly always engaging little people, she at-
tains a success enviable in any literature and in any period. The be-

lievable handling of children in stories suitable for an adult audience calls for powers of no mean order.

The prose style in *Cress Delahanty* and much of *Love Death* and *Crimson Ramblers* can best be described as Classical. This adjective would also apply to the two Jess Birdwell books if only the language there were not so deliberately rustic and dialectal. At its best, Jessamyn West's style is well husbanded, allusive, and melodious. Her prose indicates that she is much in love with words, especially with their connotations and sensuousness, and that she is conscious of the rhythmic effect of words when used singly or when strung like beads in a sentence. Yet hers is not a language of cool and alpine distances; it is warm and of the valley, full of generous feeling and aspiration, and often fragrant with a breath of passion.

It is hard to fix the distinctive manner of Jessamyn West. As valid a comparison as any is that of the early Willa Cather—without the latter's elegiac tone. The two women share much in common, including a Classical style; both of them read and admired Virgil. In developing the comparison beyond style, we may also note that they share an interest in the Midwestern pioneer and like to lay their stories in the distant past. But, whereas Miss Cather generally worked backward in time in her sequence of books, Miss West worked forward. The latter suffers in having depicted *fewer* outstanding heroic souls of the pioneer kind comparable with Ántonia Shimerda and Alexandra Bergson. Her greatest creations are two that Miss Cather, however, cannot rival: Jess and Eliza Birdwell.

III *Limitations and New Directions*

Jessamyn West's recent *A Matter of Time* and *Leafy Rivers* show that she has mastered the technical aspects of her craft and has become more Realistic than ever, yet without having advanced in any substantial way as an artist. With these books sophistication has reached its point of diminishing returns. In fact, the last novel shows quite clearly a falling off, however temporary, from the earlier triumphs. On the other hand, we cannot in fairness ask her to go on repeating herself. Probably the chief hazard she needs to beware of *is* repetition.

For examples of the repetitive quality of her fiction, we may note that the major characters in all the most important books live on or near some ranch or farm in a place strikingly like the region about North Vernon or Yorba Linda. The father is independently employed as some kind of agriculturist, asylum keeper, or garage operator. The mother, from *Witch Diggers* onward, whenever she plays any prominent role in the story, usually is more articulate and witty than her spouse; and she is also more dominant as a personality. The young married heroines either suffer from an inadequate sex education or have husbands who are sexually deficient. These two situations are, of course, common in today's dramas and novels, now that Freudianism and sex are being fully exploited. The villains who appear in Miss West's stories limit their villainy to a few things such as infidelity in marriage, sex abuse, and tyranny over women. It is almost needless to say that there are no spies, professional killers, outlaws, detectives, pirates, big-game hunters, tramps, or soldiers at war; cabaret dancers, adventuresses, saints; any foreigners whatsoever; or any of the host of other figures from the popular romances. With some notable exceptions, the world of Miss West is relatively circumscribed and domestic.

She has already discovered in the past of her ancestors and in her own girlhood what is probably her richest source of story material. But, seemingly, this vein of gold is now worked out, or has been largely abandoned in favor of claims to be found in the present time. The provocative question is whether she might have fared better had she devoted her creative energies in the beginning to either Indiana or California—instead of attenuating their effectiveness by division—and have created a whole cycle of unified novels about the frontier such as did James Fenimore Cooper, William Faulkner, and Conrad Richter. Yet this procedure would have probably left her, as it did these writers, rather restricted and repetitive.

Presumably, however, Miss West's development as a writer required the path finally taken. The Indiana past, "safe" material having nothing to do with the painful tubercular experience, helped make possible her emergence as a writer of books, especially as she could and did draw upon her mother's memories for inspiration. After she gained confidence with *Friendly Persuasion* and *Witch Diggers*, she used the more recent California past to effect a break with familial traditions, then took up her own personal experiences and moved forward, though hesitantly, into *A Matter of Time*. It is worth noting that in this late novel we see the first extended treatment of disease, the fearsome thicket which her people had long avoided except for a few minor figures like Mr. Cornelius and Mary Jessup. Maybe the ordeals of the Murphy women have at last provided the author with that final exorcism needed.

For a critic to suggest what an accomplished and mature artist should do next in her craft is hazardous if not downright presumptuous and futile. Perhaps it is forgivable to say that what Miss West needs now is a wider scope of subject that is at the same time—and this next condition is difficult for any writer to fulfill on the basis of prescription—congenial with her temperament and taste, a subject that has little or nothing to do with Vernon or Yorba Linda, or for that matter with herself or her family. This task might prove unnecessarily troublesome if she continues to follow her theory, à la Pritchett, that literature is created by examining the author's inner self, by finding out who the author is. This introspective theory leads all to easily to autobiographical results—and has done so, in her case. Fortunately, Jessamyn West is already well aware of her need to steer away henceforth from autobiography.[2]

Yet artists have forever and again colored their canvases from the paintbox of their own inimitable experience. There is no question that she has had sufficient worldly experience to furnish her with more of the raw stuff of art. She has traveled extensively in the United States and in Europe; she has known personal tragedy; she knows enough about the public school system and the university, too; she knows Hollywood; and she knows much else. Her talents brought to bear on the public schools could yield a work putting John Hersey's *The Child Buyer* to shame. And on the university, outdo Mary McCarthy's *The Groves of Academe*. Since she sees some values in Hollywood, she might have an answer to Nathanael West's grotesque *The Day of the Locust*.

She does try to broaden her scope. The brilliant *A Matter of Time* says some unconventional things for a change. Still it suffers from, among other things, an unintentional sadness and emotional withdrawal that mute whatever life celebration was supposed to emerge. Tassie Murphy herself does not, and was not intended to, communicate much of the author's joy of living. *Verzweifelungsmüt* (the courage of despair) is to the West devotee no adequate substitute for that ardent embracing of life felt over and over again in earlier stories. *Leafy Rivers* represents another commendable effort to broaden her art, to introduce that special *wildness* essential to whatever is great in literature, and to show as have the classics the power of sex in human affairs; yet, the heroine and her adventures are not sufficiently congenial to the author. As always, she makes

134

here no startling innovations in literary history when it comes to the manner of telling her story, for she is content to use such techniques as were bequeathed her by other modern writers of good reputation.

IV *Final Position*

That the scholarly presses have given so little attention to commenting on her writings is a misfortune which academic critics, who hopefully act as midwives to literary fame, may yet remedy. Meanwhile, Jessamyn West, though no longer young, is hard at work lecturing and writing; and she plans to write on into old age as Thomas Hardy did. Since art is long and criticism fleeting, it is difficult to utter at this time any final judgment of her work which can safely hope to abide the years without need of adjustment. Any day she might bring out a new book, and her new masterpiece might be celebrated in tomorrow's literary reviews. For *Crimson Ramblers* proves that she has not lost her magic.

On the basis of what has been accomplished already, it is safe to rank her as a minor artist, a biregionalist, in the literature of America, fit company for John Steinbeck and William Faulkner, Willa Cather and Eudora Welty. Several of her books—*Friendly Persuasion, Except for Me and Thee, Witch Diggers, Cress Delahanty, South of the Angels*—bear the stamp of genius. She has woven some stories of incomparable beauty; and she has made richer the imagination of millions of now loyal readers throughout the world.

Notes and References

Chapter One

1. Most of the information on Jessamyn West's parents and ancestors is taken from two West letters (August 9, 1965, and May 2, 1967) to me; to a lesser extent, from a short unpublished holograph biography of Joshua Vickers Milhous, prepared by his daughter, Marth J. Ware (original owned by Jessamyn West, as is true of family letters, letters from editors to her, and other documents used in this study unless otherwise specified). Exceptions to these two sources are cited as they occur.

2. Almira P. Milhous, *Thoughts in Verse*. With Life Sketches of Franklin and Almira P. Milhous (n.p.; c. Christmas, 1950), p. 5. Privately printed booklet of forty-four pages. Copy owned by Mrs. Allie Clark, of North Vernon, Indiana.

3. Letter from Jessamyn West (April 7, 1960) to a Mr. Mock (given name and address not specified), who had inquired about the possibility of making *The Friendly Persuasion* a kind of campaign biography of Richard M. Nixon.

4. Taken from two unnumbered pages of a 1944-45 notebook on southern Indiana farm life prepared at Jessamyn West's request by her parents. The mother's contribution, from which the nursery's name and other information on fruit are taken, occupies the first and final thirds of this notebook owned by Jessamyn West. Jess Birdwell's nursery is also called Maple Grove.

5. Letters from Grace Anna West, in Whittier, California (undated—internal evidence suggests late summer or fall, 1947) to Jessamyn West, who by that date was living in Napa. Grace's frequent talks about her Indiana past are mentioned in the letter to Mr. Mock, cited earlier.

6. "Yes" (the affirmative side of a debate with Paul Engle entitled: "Should This Father Raise His Son?") *Ladies' Home Journal*, LXXXIII (May, 1966), 149.

7. *Ibid.*, p. 151.

8. Ray Mast, " 'Friendly Persuasion' Author Recalled," Fullerton, California *News Tribune*, December 22, 1965, p. A-2.

9. From a note under photograph of West home illustrating Ray Mast's article (see note 8).

10. "Bare Hills Become Orchards as Pioneers Plan Future," *Yorba Linda Star*, October 17, 1947, p. 1. This special commemorative issue of the *Star* celebrates thirty years of the town's development and contains early photographs and articles of local history. Incidentally, during six months in 1924, West wrote society notes (unsigned) for this paper.

11. Valdo Smith, "It Took Lots of Fight to Build Yorba Linda Water Company," *Yorba Linda Star*, October 17, 1947, p. 11.

12. "Bare Hills Become Orchards. . . ."

13. Jessamyn West McPherson, " 'Those Good Old Days' by One Who Can Really Tell It," *Yorba Linda Star*, October 17, 1947, p. 1.

14. West letter (August 9, 1965) to me. The prosperity is verified in a letter from Gladys Gauldin, La Habra, California (February 7, 1967) to me. My sole but reliable evidence for the realtor business is the letterhead "Eldo R. West Representing Strout Realty Co." which is found on several letters from Grace West, *circa* 1940's.

15. West letter (January 30, 1967) to me, in which she mentions voluntarily the switching incident that is later verified for me by Gauldin (see preceding note).

16. "The Three R's," *Wilson Library Journal*, XXXI (October, 1956), 157.

17. West letters (August 9 and 18, 1965) to me. Except as otherwise noted, from these letters are taken all details concerning West's reading and tastes in this direction.

18. Lowry C. Wimberly letter (April 13, 1940) to West, in which, as editor of *Prairie Schooner*, he offers her some constructive criticism about her story.

19. West letter (May 7, 1966) to me. In a letter to her (April 8, 1940), Dudley Wynn of the *New Mexico Quarterly* said that she might become the Mary Wilkins Freeman of the 1940's, a compliment which she at that time felt to be insulting.

20. "Jessamyn West" by herself in *New York Herald Tribune Book Review*, February 18, 1951, p. 2. Edited by John K. Hutchins.

21. Recorded by Ray Mast, from an interview with Merle West. See " 'Friendly Persuasion' Author Recalled."

22. West letter (August 9, 1965) to me.

23. Whittier College transcript of Mrs. Maxwell McPherson (Jessamyn West).

24. *To See the Dream* (New York, 1957), pp. 254-55.

25. *The New Pleiades* (Fullerton Union High School and Fullerton Junior College Weekly), Vol. III (December 17, 1920), n.p.

26. Letter from Dr. William T. Boyce, Claremont, California (February 24, 1966) to me. The new library at the college was named in his honor in 1957. At the dedication ceremony, Miss West surprised everyone by donating a fairly large sum of money to establish a "William T. Boyce Fund in Creative Writing."

27. *The Pleiades*, Fullerton Union High School (1919), p. 39.

28. Letter from Mrs. Esther Lewis Mendenhall, Santa Ana, California (March 30, 1966) to me.

29. *Dream*, pp. 254-57. Also, West letter (April 8, 1966) to me; "The Three R's," p. 159.

30. Quoted by West in "Where Do Stories Come From?" *Adventures in Appreciation*, ed. Walter Loban *et al.* (New York, 1958), p. 9.

31. Transcript of grades, Whittier College.

32. "Love," *Women Today Their Conflicts, Their Frustrations and Their Fulfillments*, ed. Elizabeth Bragdon (Indianapolis, 1953), p. 87.

33. Letter from Paul S. Smith, President of Whittier College (February 9, 1966) to me.

34. "Report of a Sociology Trip to Los Angeles," by M. J. West. Copy furnished me through courtesy of Paul S. Smith, owner of the original.

35. West letter (February 4, 1966) to me.

36. Letter from Esther M. Dodson, Altadena, California (March 11, 1966) to me. Mrs. Dodson is West's cousin.

37. Letter from Richard Scowcroft, Stanford University (December 5, 1966) to me.

38. *Dream*, pp. 269-71. West letter (May 2, 1967) to me.

39. West letter (February 9, 1966) to me. The circumstances of adoption are confirmed in Boyce's letter already cited.

40. West letter (April 3, 1966) to me.

41. West letter (October 24, 1965) to me.

42. Jessamyn West, "The Trouble with Doctors Is Me," *Ladies' Home Journal*, LXXXII (March, 1965), 42, 44-45.

43. *Ibid.*, p. 45.

44. West letter (August 9, 1965) to me.

45. West letter (January 28, 1966) to me.

46. *Ibid.*

47. Xerox reproduction (owned by me) of the copy sent to Jessamyn West by her mother. Undated, but undoubtedly close to June, 1947.

48. "The Three R's," p. 159.

49. Carbon copy of a three-page, unpublished autobiography typescript (undated) that West prepared for some as yet unidentified person. Hereinafter referred to as "unpublished autobiography typescript." Copy owned by myself. Also, West letter (October 24, 1965) to me; and *Dream*, p. 258.

50. West letter (August 9, 1965) to me.

51. West letter (February 4, 1966) to me. Also, evidence in letter from Wimberly to West (April 13, 1940).

52. West letter (May 27, 1966) to me.

53. West letter (January 30, 1967) to me. Mrs. Hellen (*sic*) Ochs, of Columbus, Indiana, reports to me in two letters (May 2 and 16, 1967) of her meeting with West in 1957 at Indiana University where West was then

teaching. "She is either a shy or reticent person. . . . She was always alone."
But, "When she was approached or when a conferee had questions, needed
help, she was warm and friendly. . . . When she walked along in a corridor
or in a room she seemed to 'mentally' reach out to embrace all those around
her, actually 'sorting people' as to types." Mrs. Ochs recalls one particular
encounter that illuminates West's passion for living and her amusing sus-
ceptibility to distraction: "I went down to The Commons where the college
students eat and . . . there sat J. West with an expression of utter delight,
eating the 'gooeyest,' biggest, chocolate nut sundae, whipped cream and all,
wearing one button type earring and one long dangling one. . . . J. West
told us later that she had tried on both earrings . . . to decide which type to
wear. Something distracted her and she forgot to change."

54. Perry Miller, review in *New York Herald Tribune Book Review*,
April 15, 1962, p. 12.

55. West letter (January 30, 1967) to me.

56. The Screen Writers Guild had decided that a Michael Wilson had
written an earlier screenplay (true) which constituted a major portion of the
final script (apparently untrue). Details are in *Dream* and in Elizabeth Poe,
"Credits and Oscars," *Nation*, CLXXXIV (March 30, 1957), 267-69. West
admits that the motion-picture scene involving the man-eating females
came from Wilson's pen. But the authorship of the final shooting script,
completed on August 18, 1955, and filed by Allied Artists in the Library of
Congress, is almost completely hers and Robert Wyler's. It does not make
much sense for West to spend nine months plagiarizing from a work that
she and the Wyler brothers thought basically unsatisfactory to start with,
regardless of Wilson's alleged Communist affiliation. But the tune of the
song "Thee I Love" used in the film occurs in embryo form more than once
in the second movement of Schubert's Symphony no. 5 in B-flat major,
D. 485. Of course, West did not write the song.

57. West letter (September 7, 1965) to me.

58. *Ibid.*

59. In the essay describing the composition of "Horace Chooney, M.D."
she appears to take it for granted that the fictionist (certainly herself as one)
employs the "organic development of the narrative. . . ." *Q.v.* "The Story
of a Story," *The Pacific Spectator*, Vol. III, No. 3 (1949), p. 266.

60. *Adventures in Appreciation*, pp. 6-7.

61. Jessamyn West letter to Mr. Mock (see note 3).

62. "Story of a Story," pp. 267-68.

63. Unpublished autobiography typescript, p. 1.

64. However, see "Story of a Story," pp. 268-69.

Chapter Two

1. West letter (May 22, 1966) to me.

2. *Ibid.*

3. David Dempsey, "Talk with Jessamyn West," *New York Times Book Review*, January 3, 1954, p. 12.

4. West letter (May 7, 1966) to me.

5. *Ibid.*

6. West letter (May 22, 1966) to me.

7. West letter (January 27, 1966) to me.

8. Letter from Ken McCormick (August 8, 1941) to West. Xerox copy owned by myself.

9. West letter (May 7, 1966) to me.

10. West letter (January 26, 1966) to me.

11. Review of Jessamyn West, *The Friendly Persuasion, Saturday Review*, XXVIII (November 17, 1945), 14.

12. Review of Jessamyn West, *The Friendly Persuasion, New Mexico Quarterly*, XVII (Spring, 1947), 117.

13. (November, 1945), p. 724.

14. Complete title: *The Friend: The Quaker Weekly Journal* (November 29, 1946), p. 971. Unsigned.

15. Letter from Clarence J. Robinson, of Winchester, Pennsylvania, in *Friends Journal* (December 8, 1956), p. 791.

16. Letter from West (January 25, 1966) to me.

17. First published in *Prairie Schooner*, XIV (1940), 79-92. The other stories first appeared as follows: "Shivaree before Breakfast," *Collier's*, CXIII (January 22, 1944), 22 *et passim*; "The Pacing Goose," *Collier's*, CXVI (August 11, 1945), 36, 48-50; "Lead Her Like a Pigeon," *Atlantic Monthly*, CLXXIV (December, 1944), 60-63; "The Battle of Finney's Ford's" *Harper's Magazine*, CXCI (September, 1945), 273-84; "The Buried Leaf," *Atlantic Monthly*, CLXXVI (September, 1945), 72-76; "A Likely Exchange," *Atlantic Monthly*, CLXXIV (July, 1944), 56-61; "First Day Finish," *Atlantic Monthly*, CLXXIV (August, 1944), 88-92; " 'Yes, We'll Gather at the River,' " under the title "Carnal Room," *Collier's*, CXVI (July 21, 1945), 33, 44, 47; "The Meeting House," *Atlantic Monthly*, CLXXVI (July, 1945), 78-83; "The Vase" under the title "A Pretty Thing," *Ladies' Home Journal*, LXII (July, 1945), 35, 91, 93; "The Illumination," *Harper's Bazaar*, LXXVII (October, 1943), 101 *et passim*; "Pictures from a Clapboard House," *New Mexico Quarterly*, XV (Summer, 1945), 176 *et passim*; "Homer and the Lilies," *Ladies' Home Journal*, LXII (August, 1945), 18-19.

18. Jessamyn West, *The Friendly Persuasion* (New York, 1945), p. 8.

19. Robert B. Heilman, "Comment" on "Shivaree before Breakfast," in *Modern Short Stories A Critical Anthology* (New York, 1950), p. 108.

20. West letter (August 9, 1965) to me.

21. "And I believe that I have to some extent been handicapped in my writing by this lingering belief in the hero as [a] man who withdraws." West letter (August 18, 1965) to me.

22. "Should This Father Raise His Son?" p. 149.

23. All quoted matter as well as some other information about the sources of *Friendly Persuasion* are taken from West letter (January 26, 1966) to me. Material on Homer comes from this letter and from an undated letter written by Grace West to Jessamyn. Much information on Joshua is taken from the unpublished holograph biography of Joshua Vickers Milhous (see note 1, Chapter 1).

24. Indianapolis, 1914. Later reissued (1923) carrying the title *In the Days of My Youth. An Intimate Personal Record of Life and Manners in the Middle Ages of the Middle West.*

25. The film's success did not enhance the sales of the book, probably because the two works are so unlike. More than fifty thousand copies of the hardbound edition were sold prior to the motion picture, and almost that number afterward.—Letter from Julian P. Muller (October 13, 1965) to me.

As a rough indication of the continuing popularity of the book twenty years after first publication, the fiction librarian of the Milwaukee Public Library checked the circulation record of three *among many* copies of *Friendly Persuasion* in the Central Library and in two branches. She found that between November, 1964, and November, 1965, these selected copies had been checked out forty-three times. Of the West books, *Cress Delahanty* came second with twenty-six. —Letter from Lorraine Hartwick (November 10, 1965) to me.

The popularity of the book abroad may be roughly measured in this way: at least twenty-two editions have appeared to date in seventeen different foreign languages. —*Index Translationum*, Vols. I-XVIII; also, letter from West's literary agent, Henry Volkening (March 27, 1967) to me.

26. *Time*, LXVIII (November 5, 1956), 110, 113-14.

27. Review by "I. A. H.," *The Friend: The Quaker Weekly Journal* (November 30, 1956); review by Richmond Miller, *Friends Journal* (October 20, 1956).

28. Letter from Gladys Gauldin (May 3, 1967) to me.

29. Referred to in letter from Dudley Wynn (April 8, 1940). I own an almost complete copy of the story, thanks to the kindness of Miss West.

30. Although Miss West makes no secret at all of her having used the Jennings County Poor Farm as the setting, I on my own "discovered" the existence of the place during a search on April 22, 1966, and took some photographs which I then forwarded to Miss West. The ingenuous letter of reply from her (May 7, 1966) more than confirmed my impression. Subsequent letters from her (esp., May 30, 1967) left no doubt in my mind that here was the model.

31. West letter (January 29, 1966) to me. Also, in another letter (May 31, 1967) she writes: "I disliked Lib for instance—but the more I wrote about her the more I understood her and sympathized with her. The seeds

of the story I'm sure lie deep in my unconscious."

32. One strange example of this independence is that she did not know there was an actual cemetery connected with the Jennings County Poor Farm until I described it to her in a letter. Yet, in the novel there is one on the property within easy walking distance of the main building, and near a creek—almost precisely where the real one is! Nor did she know that the barn had once burned down, around the turn of the century, killing a colt (no people). All that we need to know are a few key pieces, she says in one of her letters to me, and then the other pieces naturally fall into place.

33. West letters (May 11 and 17, 1967) to me. Mrs. Hellen Ochs, in a letter (May 2, 1967), has kindly furnished me with copies of old North Vernon newspaper clippings that describe life at the farm shortly after the turn of this century. As the daughter-in-law of a former superintendent there, she is much impressed with the verisimilitude of *Witch Diggers*.

34. John K. Hutchins, "On an Author," *New York Herald Tribune Book Review*, February 18, 1951, p. 2.

35. Review of Jessamyn West, *The Witch Diggers*, *New York Times Book Review*, January 14, 1951, p. 5.

36. Quoted by Lee Graham, p. 24.

37. West's writing notebook (mentioned earlier) covering the years associated with the first three books, p. 56. Hereinafter referred to as "writing notebook."

38. Quoted by Dan Wyant, "Author Here for 'First Performance,'" Eugene, Oregon *Eugene Register-Guard*, May 22, 1958. Information about the production appears in a series of publicity articles published in this newspaper in May, 1958, on the following dates: 5, 16, 18, 19, 20, 21, 22, 23, 24. Also, I have used copies of pages from the *Annual Report of 1957/58* of the University Theater of Oregon, kindly furnished me by Wilhelmina Bevers (business manager). Horace W. Robinson, director of the University Theater, has supplied to me in two letters (November 4, 1965, and February 17, 1966) much additional information of an evaluative character.

39. Dan Wyant, "Premiere of Musical Is Set for Weekend," Eugene, Oregon *Eugene Register-Guard*, May 20, 1958.

40. *A Mirror for the Sky an Opera Based on an Original Conception of Raoul Péne duBois for Portraying the Life of Audubon in a Musical Drama* (New York, 1948).

41. Letter by Mrs. William J. Pease, Jr., of Eugene, printed in *Eugene Register-Guard*, May 28, 1958.

42. Quoted in letter from Mrs. Alyce R. Sheetz, of Eugene, Oregon (January 24, 1966) to me. Informant's name withheld upon request. Mrs. Sheetz is a high school journalism teacher.

43. Letter from Robinson (February 17, 1966) to me.

44. New York, 1967. The novel had the dubious honor of being abridged

for publication in *Reader's Digest*.

45. In West's letter (March 28, 1966) to me she states that she had put down *Leafy Rivers* "3/4 finished" in order to complete *A Matter of Time*, a book to which, in an earlier letter, she assigned a priority for publication. In a March 8, 1967, letter to me she confesses to having rewritten the last third of *Leafy* after it was first submitted to the publisher so that it is now "*much* improved."

46. "The book is filled with symbols."—From West letter (September 6, 1967) to me dealing with *Leafy*.

47. *Ibid*.

48. Also, see Chancellor's adverse judgment of Reno (p. 10): the schoolmaster struck him as a "careful man," one who "wouldn't take a chance."

49. West letter (September 6, 1967) to me.

50. *Ibid*.

51. West letter (May 22, 1966) to me.

Chapter Three

1. This novel, despite its late position among her published books, was conceived early—within a few years of the composition of *Witch Diggers*. Miss West says the germinal idea found in the writing notebook was recorded about fifteen to twenty years before *Leafy Rivers* was published.

2. Included in *Cross Section 1948* [:] *A Collection of New American Writing*, ed. by Edwin Seaver (New York, 1948), pp. 1-96.

3. Original title: "Little Men," included in *Star Short Novels*, ed. by Frederik Pohl (New York, 1954), reprinted in book-length form as *The Chilekings* (New York, 1967). Both are paperbound editions.

4. The separate stories were first published as follows: "A Time of Learning," *Ladies' Home Journal*, LXIII (March, 1946), 26-27, 194, 196-97, 199; "The Mysteries of Life in an Orderly Manner," *New Yorker*, XXIV (March 27, 1948), 29-30; "Love, Death, and the Ladies' Drill Team," *New Yorker*, XXVII (September 22, 1951), 33-37; "Homecoming," *American Prefaces*, IV (Summer, 1939), 164-67; "The Battle of the Suits," *New Yorker*, XXX (February 5, 1955), 32-36; "Tom Wolfe's My Name," *New Mexico Quarterly*, XIV (Summer, 1944), 153-65; "Learn to Say Good-bye" under the title "The Lesson," *New Yorker*, XXVII (August 11, 1951), 25-30; "A Little Collar for the Monkey" under the title "A Gift for the Bride's Mother," *Woman's Home Companion*, LXXV (February, 1948), 30 *et passim*; "Public Address System," *Harper's Magazine*, CXCVII (October, 1948), 93-102; "Foot-Shaped Shoes" under the title "You've Got to Grow Up Sometime," *Saturday Evening Post*, CCXXVII (March 12, 1955), 31, 80-81, 84-85, 87; "Horace Chooney, M.D.," *Mademoiselle*, XXIV (February, 1947), 225, 302-7; "The Linden Trees," *The Tanager, a Quarterly Review*, XVIII (February, 1943), 3-8; "Breach of Promise," *Harper's Magazine*, CCVI (April,

1953), 46-57; "The Singing Lesson," *Harper's Magazine*, CXC (January, 1945), 145-50.

5. October 16, 1955, p. 4.

6. *Love Death and the Ladies' Drill Team* (New York, 1955), p. 27.

7. "West's LOVE, DEATH AND THE LADIES' DRILL TEAM," *The Explicator*, XXIII (December, 1964), item 27.

8. Edward C. Aswell, "A Note on Thomas Wolfe," *The Hills Beyond*, by Thomas Wolfe (New York, 1964), p. 146.

9. West letter (September 7, 1965) to me: "I can't think *what* Harrison Smith was thinking about when he wrote of Dr. Chooney. His version of the story came out of *his* head, not out of my narrative. Your interpretation is the right one."

10. *Cress Delahanty* (New York, 1953). The separate stories here were first published in altered form under these titles (following the sequence of the sixteen in the book): "The Child's Day," *New Mexico Quarterly*, X (Winter, 1940), 233 *et seq.*; "The Mush Pot," *Foothills*, I (Winter, 1939), six unnumbered pages; "Mr. Powers," *New Yorker*, XXIV (July 24, 1948), 24-26; "The Hat," *Ladies' Home Journal*, LXV (May, 1948), 46-47, 141-44, 146; "Recapitulation," *Ladies' Home Journal*, LXVIII (October, 1951), 53, 239-40, 243-45; "Road to the Isles," *New Yorker*, XXIII (February 21, 1948), 27-30; "A Few Lines for Mrs. Charlesbois," *Woman's Day*, 16th Year, 3rd issue (December, 1952), 52-53, 106-19; "Arma Virumque Cano," *Harper's Magazine*, CIIC (January, 1949), 72-77; "The Sump Hole," *New Yorker*, XXII (December 14, 1946), 39-44; "King Midas in Reverse," *Colorado Quarterly*, I (Summer, 1952), 58-66; "Summer of Signs and Portents," *New Yorker*, XXIV (August 28, 1948), 21-25; the two stories corresponding to "Fourteen: Summer II" and "Fourteen: Spring" have not been located yet; "You Can't Talk about It," *Ladies' Home Journal*, LXX (July, 1953), 28, 74-76; "Mr. Cornelius, I Love You," *Collier's*, CXXX (November 22, 1952), 20-21 *et passim*; "Grandpa Was Her Mirror," *Harper's Magazine*, CXCII (May, 1946), 439-42.

11. Thomas Huzzell, *The Techniques of the Novel* (New York, 1959), p, 47. Paperbound edition.

12. West in *Adventures in Appreciation*, p. 8.

13. Boyce Letter (February 24, 1966) to me.

14. West letter (March 28, 1966) to me.

15. West letter (February 9, 1966) to me.

16. Jessamyn West, "Grandpa Was Her Mirror," *Harper's Magazine*, CXCII (May, 1946), 442.

17. Boyce, *loc. cit.*

18. David Dempsey, "Talk with Jessamyn West."

19. New York, 1960.

20. The composition of *South of the Angels* must have begun not much earlier than February, 1956; for at that time Miss West still considered the

work a "new" one. But she was far enough along to regard the Copes as the main people. See *Dream*, p. 4.

21. Gauldin letter (February 7, 1967) to me.

22. Valdo Smith. Incidentally, a short story that was reworked and made part of the novel is "The Leppert," *Senior Scholastic*, XXXXVI (April 23, 1945), 21-22, 28-30.

23. Tuberculosis (herself, an uncle, and a cousin); cancer (Grace West, Carmen, and three grandparents—the last four of these having died of it—plus Eldo West); crippling arthritis (Myron); migraine (herself).

24. *Dream*, p. 88. But this was far from being the first time. She says in her article "Jessamyn West," *New York Herald Tribune Book Review*, February 18, 1951, p. 2, that she had read Thoreau and his notebooks "more often than any other writer. . . ." The first entry in her writing notebook consists of a short quote from him describing fireflies ("bronze light").

25. *Love Is Not What You Think* (New York, 1959).

26. Original title of West's manuscript which, after she had shortened it, became *A Matter of Time* (New York, 1966).

27. West letters (May 22 and October 10, 1966) to me.

28. In West's story "Love" there is a second Reverdy who, like the first one in 1943, has an unfortunate childhood. The husband of this later Reverdy is also named Everett. Like Tassie and Blix, she has a severe illness, and has already gone through several marriages presumably because of false, prudish attitudes toward sexual love. But unlike Tassie, she comes to realize, finally, but too late, that love is of the flesh as well as of the spirit.

29. "A Gentle Storyteller Challenges Death," *Life*, LXI (October 21, 1966), 8.

30. Quoted by Lee Graham, p. 26.

31. Interestingly enough, however, Rita Estok in *Library Journal* (October 1, 1966) was one of the few reviewers who objected openly to the idea of euthanasia. In my own coverage in *Saturday Review* (October 22, 1966), I did not mention my own objection, taking it for granted that West was inviting a good deal of opposition, expressed or otherwise. Perhaps my omission did not matter, for in West's interview with Lee Graham, published later, she disavowed advocating any general practice of euthanasia; she simply stated that Blix had a right to decide for herself.

32. West letter (May 22, 1966) to me. Earlier, Julian Muller in a letter (February 17, 1966) to me wrote that West was at that time performing "extensive revisions" in the work.

33. West letter (October 10, 1966) to me.

34. My autographed copy of Charles Cooper's *Whittier: Independent College in California*, containing a preface by West, is inscribed in her handwriting: "For Alfred Shivers, who knows Pilgrim College and therefore will not find this strange."

35. "I want to say that Jessamyn's love and devotion for her immediate

family—father, mother, brother has been impressive. I think she must have had a most happy home life."—Letter from Dr. Boyce (February 24, 1966) to me.

36. *Crimson Ramblers of the World, Farewell* (New York, 1970). All comments made on the stories are based, however, on a reading of the galleys and of course the earlier magazine versions of the stories, for at the time of this writing the book per se had yet to appear. The stories were originally published as follows, with the exception of those labeled "new" which made their first appearance in *Crimson Ramblers*: "Up a Tree" (new); "There Ought to Be a Judge," *Mademoiselle*, XXIII (June, 1946), 134-35, 212-17; "Gallup Poll" formerly titled "The Love Ballot," *American Magazine*, CXL (August, 1945), 42-43; "Alive and Well," *Harper's Bazaar*, No. 2829, 81st yr. (September, 1947), 223, 266, 268, 270; "I'll Ask Him to Come Sooner," *The Tanager, A Bi-Monthly Review*, XII (December, 1941), 9-16; "Hunting for Hoot Owls," *Harper's Magazine*, CCXXVIII (January, 1964), 86-94; "Crimson Ramblers of the World, Farewell" (new); "Night Piece for Julia," *Rocky Mountain Review*, VIII (Fall, 1943), 10-12; "Live Life Deeply" (new); "Mother's Day," *New Yorker*, XLVI (May 30, 1970), 32-37; "The Heavy Stone," *American Magazine*, CXLV (March, 1948), 22-23, 126, 128-30; "99.6," *Broun's Nutmeg*, III (June 10, 1939), 7; "The Day of the Hawk," *Foothills*, I (Fall, 1939), nine unnumbered pages; "Like Visitant of Air," details of magazine publication uncertain, but story anthologized in *Modern Reading*, 14, edited by Reginald A. More (London, 1941-46); "The Condemned Librarian," *Harper's Magazine*, CCXI (July, 1955), 45-53; "Child of the Century," *Woman's Day*, 16th yr., 2nd issue (November, 1952), 54 *et seq.*

37. West letter (August 28, 1970) to me.

38. *Ibid.*

39. *Ibid.*

40. *Yale Review*, New Series, XXXIX (December, 1949), 255-62.

41. *Town and Country*, C (November, 1945), 124, 152, 154, 156, 159. Reprinted in *O. Henry Memorial Award Prize Stories of 1946*, edited by Herschel Brickell and Muriel Fuller (Garden City, New York, 1946).

Chapter Four

1. *Wedded in Prison* (London, 1925).

2. In a letter to me (December 20, 1966) during the season that *A Matter of Time* was first appearing on the market, Miss West wrote about her future plans for books: ". . . leaving the autobiographical out (*sic*) this is the way I think I should go."

Selected Bibliography

PRIMARY SOURCES

As the poems are not discussed in this study, they are not listed here. The twenty-six that have been located were published as follows: *Commonweal* (1943-44, 1954), *The Tanager* (1943), *New Mexico Quarterly* (1943), *Direction* (1944), *Harper's Bazaar* (1944-45), *New Yorker* (1947-48), and *Ladies' Home Journal* (1950-54). Only those short stories are listed which have not as yet been collected by Miss West or reworked by her into some book. For those stories which have gone into her books, see the appropriate entries in the Notes and References section.

1. Books

The Friendly Persuasion. New York: Harcourt, Brace and Company, 1945.
A Mirror for the Sky An Opera Based on an Original Conception of Raoul Péne duBois for Portraying the Life of Audubon in a Musical Drama. Costume sketches by Raoul Péne duBois. New York: Harcourt, Brace and Company, 1948.
The Witch Diggers. New York: Harcourt, Brace and Company, 1951.
The Reading Public. New York: Harcourt, Brace and Company, 1952. Privately printed for her friends and publishers.
Cress Delahanty. New York: Harcourt, Brace & World, 1953.
Love Death and the Ladies' Drill Team. New York: Harcourt, Brace & World, 1955.
To See the Dream. New York: Harcourt, Brace & World, 1957.
Love Is Not What You Think. New York: Harcourt, Brace & World, 1959.
South of the Angels. New York: Harcourt, Brace & World, 1960.
The Quaker Reader. Selected and introduced by Jessamyn West. New York: The Viking Press, 1962.
A Matter of Time. New York: Harcourt, Brace & World, 1966.
The Chilekings. New York: Ballantine Books, 1967. Reprint of *Little Men* first published in *Star Short Novels*, edited by Frederik Pohl for Ballantine Books in 1954.
Leafy Rivers. New York: Harcourt, Brace & World, 1967.
Except for Me and Thee. New York: Harcourt, Brace & World, 1967.
Crimson Ramblers of the World, Farewell. New York: Harcourt Brace Jovanovich, 1970.

149

2. Uncollected Stories

"Footprints beneath the Snow." Written about 1940, this is one of her unpublished stories. Pp. 22. Original owned by West.

"Flow Gently Sweet Aspirin," *New Masses*, XXXVIII (January 21, 1941), 13, 15.

"The Snow Is Dancing," *Yankee*, VII (January, 1941), 11-12.

"The Stove that Had the Devil in It," *Decade of Short Stories*, III (November-December, 1941), 32-39.

"Reverdy," *New Mexico Quarterly*, XIII (Spring, 1943), 21 *et seq.*

"A Little Walk with Brother," *Woman's Home Companion*, LXXXI (September, 1945), 21, 100, 102-3.

"The Wake," *Town and Country*, C (October, 1945), 136, 166, 168-70.

"The Blackboard," *Town and Country*, C (November, 1945), 124, 152, 154, 156, 159. Reprinted in *O. Henry Memorial Award Prize Stories of 1946.*

"Presumed Missing," *Mademoiselle*, XXII (January, 1946), 130, 232-36.

"Spring of Life," *American Magazine*, CXXXXI (April, 1946), 50-51, 136-39.

"There'll Come a Day," *Collier's*, CXVII (May 11, 1946), 11, 61-64.

"Grand Opening," *Ladies' Home Journal*, LXIII (September, 1946), 20-21, 150-54, 156-57.

"Another Word Entirely," *New Mexico Quarterly*, XVII (Spring, 1947), 63-71.

"The Pismire Plan," *Cross Section 1948* [:] *A Collection of New American Writing*. Edited by Edwin Seaver. New York: Simon and Schuster, 1948. Pp. 1-96.

"Perigord," *Ladies' Home Journal*, LXV (January, 1948), 50-51, 140-41.

"The Beckoning Years," *Ladies' Home Journal*, LX (May, 1949), 58-59, 237-38, 241-45, 247.

"Love," *Ladies' Home Journal*, LXVI (September, 1949), 68-69 *et passim.*

"The Ouija Board," *Yale Review*, New Series, XXXIX (December, 1949), 255-62.

"Search for Tomorrow," *Good Housekeeping*, CLIV (June, 1962), 65, 154, 156-58, 160.

"The Last Laugh," *Redbook*, CXIX (July, 1962), 50-51, 92-97.

"In Search of a Kiss," *Good Housekeeping*, CLVI (June, 1963), 76, 133-34, 136, 138.

"For One Golden Moment," *Good Housekeeping*, CLVII (November, 1963), 79 *et passim.*

"Good-bye, Bossy," *Ladies' Home Journal*, LXXXII (June, 1965), 82-83, 107-10.

3. Articles, Speeches, and Introductories

"Meet an Overseas War Bride," *Ladies' Home Journal*, LXII (August, 1946), 127-32, 194.

Selected Bibliography

" 'Those Good Old Days' by One Who Can Really Tell It," *Yorba Linda Star*, October 17, 1947. P. 1.

"Story of a Story," *The Pacific Spectator*, III (Summer, 1949), 264-73.

"Home for Christmas," *Mademoiselle*, XXIX (December, 1949), 52, 120-24, 129, 131-32. Not to be confused with the short story by that name in *Except for Me and Thee*.

"Jessamyn West," *New York Herald Tribune Book Review*, February 18, 1951. P. 2. Edited by John K. Hutchens.

————. *New York Herald Tribune Book Review*, October 7, 1951. P. 18.

"Is Love Enough?" *Mademoiselle*, XXXVI (February, 1953), 100, 166-70.

"Live Where You Are," *Mademoiselle*, XXXVIII (January, 1954), 68, 128-29.

"Four Years—for What?" *Addresses by Richard Nixon and Jessamyn West*. Whittier College *Bulletin*, XLVII. December, 1954. Pp. 15-24.

"The Choice of Greatness," *Journal of the American Association of University Women*, IL (January, 1956), 82-84.

"West, A Place to Hang Your Dreams," *Woman's Home Companion*, LXXXIII (May, 1956), 46-47.

"The Three R's," *Wilson Library Bulletin*, XXXI (October, 1956), 155-59.

"Hollywood Diary," *Ladies' Home Journal*, LXXIII (November, 1956), 70-71 *et passim*. Condensation of *To See the Dream*.

"Secret of the Masters," *Saturday Review*, XL (September 21, 1957), 13-14, 44.

"The Slave Cast Out," *Living Novel*. Edited by Granville Hicks. New York: Macmillan, 1957. Pp. 194-211.

"Where Do Stories Come From?" *Adventures in Appreciation*. Edited by Walter Loban, Dorothy Holstrom, Luella B. Cook and Herbert Potell (reading consultant). New York: Harcourt, Brace & Company, 1958. Pp. 1-13.

"On Words and Men," *Jessamyn West on Words and Men Richard Nixon The Independent College*. Whittier College *Bulletin*, LIII. May, 1960. Pp. 1-12. Speech.

Foreword. *Letters of a Woman Homesteader*. By Elinore Pruitt Stewart. Lincoln, Nebraska: University of Nebraska Press, 1961. Pp. v-vii.

"Violence," *Redbook*, CXX (January, 1963), 35, 104-5.

"On Friendship between Women," *Holiday*, XXXV (March, 1964), 13-17.

"Prelude to Tragedy," *Redbook*, CXXIII (July, 1964), 53, 84-92.

"The Trouble with Doctors Is Me," *Ladies' Home Journal*, LXXXII (March, 1965), 42, 44, 46. Contains autobiography.

"Yes." Part of debate with Paul Engle on the question: "Should This Father Raise His Son?" *Ladies' Home Journal*, LXXXIII (May, 1966), 88 *et passim*. Contains autobiography.

"Her Unmistakeable Style." West's contribution to a symposium entitled: "The California Woman." *Ladies' Home Journal*, LXXXIV (July,

1967), 76, 115-16.

Preface to *Whittier: Independent College in California*, by Charles W. Cooper. Los Angeles: Ward Ritchie Press, 1967. Pp. ix-xvii. Contains autobiography.

"Getting Personal," *The PTA Magazine*, LXIII (September, 1968), 5-7.

"Jessamyn West Talks about Her Cousin President Nixon," *McCall's*, XCVI (February, 1969), 69-70. Contains description of Yorba Linda and some material on family background.

"The Good Life on Earth," a symposium by Jessamyn West, Jean Stafford, M. F. K. Fisher *et al.* in *McCall's*, XCVII (January, 1970), 29-38, 95.

"On the River" (article included in this column), edited by "Grandma" Sue Lucas, *The Parker Pioneer* (Parker, Arizona), March 5, 1970. P. 4.

"Marina Oswald Porter: Seven Years after Dallas," *Redbook*, CXXXV (August, 1970), 57-59, 129-32, 134-35.

"Toward Peace," *Redbook*; CXXXV (September, 1970), 75, 131, 133, 135, 137, 139.

4. *Letters and Miscellaneous*

The great majority of the following West letters to Alfred S. Shivers deal in some way with autobiography or explication of stories and novels or bibliographical problems. Save for excerpts herein, none of the West correspondence has yet been published.

Letters written in *1965*: July 15; August 9, 18; September 7; October 24; *1966*: January 20, 25, 26 (last two in same envelope), 27, 28, 29; February 1, 4, 5 (last two in same envelope), 9; March 28; April 3, 8 (last two in same envelope); May 7, 17, 22, 24, 26, 27, June 20; October 10; December 17 (note on Christmas card), 20; *1967*: January 30; February 18; March 8, 16, 20; April 12; May 2, 11, 17, 22, 25, 27, 30 (these foregoing May letters reject claims made by Hellen Ochs that *Witch Diggers* was heavily indebted to actual persons and situations at the Poor Farm), 31; September 6, 29; October 23; *1969*: December 17; *1970*: August 4, 28.

Unpublished writing notebook. 175 pp. Covers *Friendly Persuasion* and *Witch Diggers* writing period. Entries largely undated. Original owned by West, along with several other writing notebooks.

Unpublished three-page autobiography typescript (undated). Carbon copy owned by Alfred S. Shivers, courtesy of Miss West.

"Report of a Sociology Trip to Los Angeles," by M. J. West. Written for Professor Paul S. Smith's class, Whittier College school year 1922-23. Original owned by Smith.

1944-45 notebook on Southern Indiana farm life prepared at Jessamyn West's request by her parents. Unnumbered pages. Owned by Jessamyn West. Although not showing any direct sources for story plots, it gives a firsthand account of everyday domestic life and furnishes the kind of concrete detail that might have stimulated West's imagination.

Selected Bibliography

SECONDARY SOURCES

I. *Items about Jessamyn West*

BERGLER, EDMUND. "Writers of Half Talent." *American Imago*, XIV (Summer, 1957), 155-64. Bergler, an M.D., writes a remarkably stuffy, biased coverage of *Witch Diggers* that claims West ought to have delved deeply into the psychic disorders of just about everyone at the Poor Farm, i.e., write clinical cases, apparently at the expense of literature.

DEMPSEY, DAVID. "Talk with Jessamyn West." *New York Times Book Review*, January 3, 1954. P. 12. Accurate though very short, rambling survey of West as a person and as a writer. He makes a few remarks—evidently derived from the author herself—on the writing techniques up to the time of *Cress Delahanty*.

GRAHAM, LEE. "An Interview with Jessamyn West." *Writer's Digest*, XLVII (May, 1967), 24-27. Contains some useful information about the author's intentions in *A Matter of Time* and about her writing in general.

HAVIGURST, WALTER. Comment on "Mr. Cornelius, I Love You." Instructor's manual for *Masters of the Modern Short Story*. New Edition. New York: Harcourt, Brace & World, 1953. Pp. 34-35. Like practically all explications of West's stories, this one is quite short and is intended for school instruction. Moderate value.

HEILMAN, ROBERT B. Comment on "Shivaree before Breakfast." *Modern Short Stories A Critical Anthology*. New York: Harcourt, Brace and Company, 1950. Pp. 107-8. Analysis is brief but perceptive.

KATOPE, CHRISTOPHER G. "West's LOVE, DEATH AND THE LADIES' DRILL TEAM.'" *Explicator*, XXIII (December, 1964), item 27. Except for its note of optimism concerning the heroine's final state of mind, this little explication alluding to Shelley's "Ode to the West Wind" is highly interesting and easy to follow.

KEMPTON, KENNETH PAYSON. Comment on "Love, Death and the Ladies' Drill Team." *Short Stories for Study*. Cambridge, Massachusetts: Harvard University Press, 1953. Mentions the wind symbolism elaborated on by Katope later; contains a few questionable assumptions that detract from the value of the explication. For instance, Imola's "childhood environment" does not seem to have been far away; it is only her lover who is referred to as being a "Mexican." Also, there is nothing indicating that Emily and John love each other—in fact, the earlier story in *Love Death* collection suggests strongly that they do not get along well together.

KING, BRENDA. "Jessamyn West," *Saturday Review*, XL (September 21, 1957), 14. Interesting as one of the earliest printed articles devoted to West the writer.

MAST, RAY. "'Friendly Persuasion' Author Recalled." Fullerton, California

153

News Tribune, December 22, 1965, p. A-2. Valuable material about West's childhood in Yorba Linda. But see letter from West to editor in The Mailbag, *News Tribune,* January 17, 1966, p. A-7, correcting some statements made about her in the Mast article.

"Noted Author Gives FJC Scholarship Fund." [Unsigned] Fullerton, California *News Tribune,* October 21, 1957, pt. 1, p. 1. Reports how West honored her old teacher, Dr. William T. Boyce, in setting up a fund in his name awarding prize money to students in creative writing.

"The Week's Work." [Unsigned] *Collier's,* CXVI (August 11, 1945), 80. A tiny portion of this article tells about the life and writings of West up to 1945; it deals with her ancestry, studies at Oxford, and her attempt to get her first story accepted by the *Hairenik Weekly.*

"WEST, JESSAMYN." *The Oxford Companion to American Literature.* Ed. by James D. Hart. 4th ed. New York: Oxford University Press, 1965. P. 906. The birthdate here, as in other publications, is in error. Brief statement, but generous tone.

——— *The Reader's Encyclopedia of American Literature.* Ed. by Max J. Herzberg *et al.* New York: Thomas Y. Crowell, 1962. P. 1211. Errs in stating that West began writing in the sanatorium and that practically all the books following *Friendly Persuasion* received "similar accolades."

——— *Twentieth Century American Authors.* Ed. by Stanley J. Kunitz and Vineta Colby. First Supplement. New York: H. W. Wilson, 1955. Biographical treatment is short but friendly; about as factually accurate as one is likely to find among library research tools.

2. *Background*

ASWELL, EDWARD C. "A Note on Thomas Wolfe." Thomas Wolfe. *The Hills Beyond.* New York: Harper & Row "Perennial Library," 1964. Aswell's statement that Wolfe did not write his later books in ledgers might interest someone who reads "Tom Wolfe's My Name."

BALDWIN, JAMES. *In My Youth from the Posthumous Papers of Robert Dudley.* Indianapolis: Bobbs-Merrill Company, 1914. An autobiographical novel giving insight into the life of Indiana Quakers at about the time of Jess Birdwell.

BANTA, RICHARD E. *Indiana Authors and Their Books, 1816-1916.* Crawfordsville, Indiana: Wabash College, 1949. Still useful pioneer study that has been superseded by Shumaker's (see below).

COOPER, CHARLES W. *Whittier: Independent College in California.* Los Angeles: Ward Ritchie Press, 1967. History of the college from its founding; contains much miscellaneous information on the teachers and famous alumni of West's generation. The preface by West describes the school of her day as being much like "Pilgrim College," save for a handful of superb teachers.

154

Selected Bibliography

HINTZ, HOWARD WILLIAM. *The Quaker Influence in American Literature*. New York: Fleming H. Revell, 1940. Excellent on early literary figures; ignores those after Whittier and Whitman.

JONES, RUFUS M. *The Quakers in the American Colonies*. New York: Macmillan, 1911. Broad, scholarly survey covering the Quakers and their roles in New England, New York, Pennsylvania, and the southern colonies.

———— *The Faith and Practice of the Quakers*. New York: Harper Bros., 1927. Relatively short but lucid account of the beliefs and practices of Friends.

MILHOUS, ALMIRA P. *Thoughts in Verse*. With Life Sketches of Franklin and Almira P. Milhous. Privately printed booklet of forty-four pages. No details of publication listed; but printed *circa* Christmas, 1950. Copy owned by Mrs. Allie Clark of North Vernon, Indiana. The chief value of this pamphlet consists of details about the Milhous family history.

RUSSELL, ELBERT. *The History of Quakerism*. New York: Macmillan, 1942. Treatment of Quakerism as a whole, starting with 1647 and running up to World War II, based partly upon the famous "Rowntree Series" of Quaker histories plus more recent additions to the knowledge of Quaker history.

SHUMAKER, ARTHUR W. *A History of Indiana Literature with Emphasis on the Authors of Imaginative Works Who Commenced Writing Prior to World War II*. Indianapolis: Indiana Historical Society, 1962. Careful, apparently exhaustive coverage of Indiana authors; arranged according to the types of literature produced; contains short appraisals. West is omitted.

TRUEBLOOD, DAVID ELTON. *The People Called the Quakers*. New York: Harper & Row, 1966. Philosophical, not historical account; has chapter about Quaker authors, older ones *and* moderns, but best about older ones.

Index

157

Index